About the Author

Michael Holley is the author of three *New York Times* bestsellers, including *Patriot Reign* and *Never Give Up*. He was a *Boston Globe* sportswriter for ten years and currently co-hosts *The Dale & Holley Show* on Boston sports radio station WEEI. He lives in Boston with his wife.

RED SOX RULE

Also by Michael Holley

Patriot Reign

RED SOX RULE

TERRY FRANCONA
AND BOSTON'S RISE
TO DOMINANCE

Michael Holley

HARPER

NEW YORK • LONDON • TORONTO • SYDNEY

HARPER

A hardcover edition of this book was published in 2008 by HarperEntertainment, an imprint of HarperCollins Publishers.

RED SOX RULE. Copyright © 2008 by Michael Holley. All rights reserved. Printed in the United States of America. No part of this book may be used or reproduced in any manner whatsoever without written permission except in the case of brief quotations embodied in critical articles and reviews. For information address HarperCollins Publishers, 10 East 53rd Street, New York, NY 10022.

HarperCollins books may be purchased for educational, business, or sales promotional use. For information please write: Special Markets Department, HarperCollins Publishers, 10 East 53rd Street, New York, NY 10022.

FIRST HARPER PAPERBACK PUBLISHED 2009.

Designed by Renato Stanisic

The Library of Congress has catalogued the hardcover edition as follows:
Holley, Michael.
    Red Sox rule : Terry Francona and Boston's rise to dominance / Michael
    Holley.—1st ed.
        207 p., [8] p. of plates : ill. ; 24 cm.
        ISBN 978-0-06-145854-5
        1. Francona, Terry, 1959–. 2. Boston Red Sox (Baseball team). 3. Baseball
        managers—Massachusetts—Boston. I. Title.
GV875.B62 H65 2008
796.357'640974461 22   2008001732

ISBN 978-0-06-145855-2 (pbk.)

09 10 11 12 13 WBC/RRD 10 9 8 7 6 5 4 3 2 1

For Oni,
The best manager of all:
you managed my life
when I was too busy to do it myself

Contents

The Hub

When you live in Boston, you learn over time to accept the city's quirks. You become so well adjusted that after a while, you don't refer to them as quirks at all. What seems odd about the city to an outsider is simply cliché—*That's just the way it is*—to a Bostonian. So you get used to streets that are confusing enough to put your GPS on the fritz: there are multiple streets with the same names and streets that change names without warning, and that's assuming you caught the name in the first place. You get used to the contradiction of being in a city of 600,000 residents that still feels like a small town when people get to talking; in Boston, everyone either has a "guy" with political and social connections or they know a guy who knows a guy.

There are the five dozen traffic circles that you learn to navigate. There's the democracy—Grandma knows some obscene gestures, too—that you come to expect while driving. There's the irony of such a small piece of land having so many territorial lines drawn into it. You can drive for just 3 miles and 12 minutes and travel through a republic (Cambridge), a town (Brookline), and a city

(Boston). There's the distinct accent, made famous by Kennedys and townies alike, where *shots* have nothing to do with tequila. Rather, *shots* are what you wear when it's just too hot for pants. And in an area where a walk down Massachusetts Avenue will take you past the Berklee College of Music, MIT, and Harvard, there's the future you get used to seeing when you stare into the faces of 19-year-old kids: they could easily be the next Quincy Jones, the next NASA recruits, or the next well-known politicians who inspire you, for better or worse, to protest with a bumper sticker.

Like many cities, Boston has a major league baseball team. But that's where the comparisons to other cities begin and end. New York, Chicago, and Los Angeles have two teams apiece, so they have built-in checks and balances that prevent them from being as locked in on one team as Boston is on the Red Sox. Besides, those cities, with massive populations and large amounts of land, have enough room to literally and figuratively get lost in. The dazzle and intrigue of Hollywood can easily compete with and trump the accomplishments of the Dodgers and Angels. The sheer bigness, coolness, and "nowness" of New York City guarantee that whenever the Yankees and Mets have the city's spotlight, that spotlight is seasonal. And Chicago is so big that it could hold two or three Bostons on its shoulders without flinching from the extra weight.

Then there is Boston, the smallest big city in the United States. There are no hiding places here in the city that writer Oliver Wendell Holmes once nicknamed "the Hub of the solar system." Fenway Park and the city have so much in common—compact, old, unique—that it often seems that one blends into the other. Neither park nor city has much sympathy for the claustrophobic. Fenway, baseball's smallest and oldest park, has the sport's longest streak of consecutive sellouts: the park hasn't had a single vacancy in 388 home games, or nearly 5 seasons. People will pay $20 just to stand behind those who actually have seats on game days. Some will pay twice that amount for the right to sit directly behind a giant green pole (the seat is so bad that it makes the already euphemistic phrase "obstructed view" seem misleading).

In tiny Fenway, the Red Sox, Boston's Hollywood summer stars, are always being watched and judged by someone. The team's press corps is enormous, which means that players and management truly have to be close to the media, whether they like it or not. At least 50 media members cover the team away from home, with that number sometimes swelling to 75. Give or take a reporter and it means that the size of the Red Sox's *road* press contingent is similar to that of the group of White House correspondents who cover the President daily. The media numbers get sillier when the Red Sox are at home, when at least 135 to 150 media members show up, even when the Red Sox are playing the worst teams in the league. Last spring, the team issued 300 credentials to those who planned to cover parts of spring training in Fort Myers, Florida.

The coverage is a constant reminder of the obvious in New England, and that is that everyone always has something to say about the team. Always. Despite the crowds in the stands as well as in the press box, it's not clear whether the baseball conversation *begins* at Fenway or simply is *continued* there.

"Somewhere along the line it got to the point where the Red Sox weren't an option," says Theo Epstein, the Boston-raised general manager of the Red Sox. "It's not an elective; it's a staple. It's a tradition that's more common than a family dinner."

There is no such thing as a no-baseball zone in Boston. The game is dissected in places that you would expect, such as sports bars, by people you would expect, such as males between the ages of 25 and 54, also known as the dream men for advertisers. But the dissection is so widespread that the demographics can't quite capture it. The manager of the Red Sox, Terry Francona, arrived at work one day last summer and found a message from a ranting e-mailer in his in-box. The writer profanely explained why Francona was a "moron" and most responsible for a regular-season loss. The criticism didn't surprise him as much as the institution from which it was sent: Harvard.

The gift and curse of the Red Sox is that they belong to everybody. They are claimed by Ivy League professors and intellectuals, by Oscar-winning actors and bestselling authors, by working women and stay-at-home moms, by those who practice the law and those who wind up on the wrong side of it. The gift is that instead of being pulled in one direction to represent a certain community or agenda, the Red Sox are surrounded by all those interests, which forms a circle. Which is also the curse: there is nothing carefree and loose about this group hug. It's expressive and intense, a passionate embrace that won't let go.

Here, asking someone about the Red Sox is like asking them if they have the time. The assumption is that they at least know what happened in last night's game, who's pitching tonight, and precisely where the Yankees are in the standings. And really, those are just the superficial talking points for short elevator rides. The real conversation, the one with substance, feels more like an heirloom. It's an in-progress discussion, a thread that began in the early 1900s that each Red Sox generation tweaks and maintains.

What it means for contemporary Red Sox management and players is this: the team's average fan is an oral historian. The city is full of fans who can seemingly walk and Google at the same time, people who can instantly connect a Red Sox slump in 2007 to the team's historic one in 1978. This is a place where names are loaded. Harry Frazee. Tom Yawkey. Bucky Dent. Bill Buckner. Grady Little. This is a place where *years* are loaded. 1918, when the

Red Sox sold Babe Ruth to the Yankees. 1978. 1986. 2003. Of course, it's a given that it's a place whose unforgivable baseball sins usually have something to do with New York—either losing a divisional lead to the Yankees, losing any series to the Yankees, leaving to play for the Yankees, or wearing a Yankees hat.

The city's natural voice is animated and coarse. You don't have to wait for poll results to know if you're loved or hated. If you're a member of the Red Sox, you can be loved and despised in the same week. Or game. Outside of Fenway, the city pushes you to be faster. Drive faster. Talk faster. Think faster. Move faster. At Fenway, the microcosm of the city pushes you to be better. Hit better. Run better. Draft better. Manage better.

When the Red Sox are successful, that pushing is called passion and Fenway is paradise. In seasons that end without an appearance in the playoffs, those players and managers who might seek an escape from baseball in the city find that such an escape doesn't exist.

Jerry Remy, who played for the Angels and Red Sox in his 10-year career, has seen the city's baseball obsession from all angles. He grew up in Somerset, 50 miles from Fenway. He spent the final seven seasons of his career as a Red Sox second baseman. He briefly thought of coaching and managing the Red Sox's Triple-A team in Pawtucket, Rhode Island. And for the last 20 years, he has watched nearly every game in his role as analyst on the team's television network.

"There's something about this city that some players can handle and some can't," Remy says. "It's the idea of 'comfort.' Here, you had better not get too comfortable. This city will make you uncomfortable."

Remy mentioned Fred Lynn, a former teammate who finished his first Red Sox season in 1975 as American League Rookie of the Year and Most Valuable Player. "This city pushed him to another level. I always tell people that if he had played his entire career here, he'd be in the Hall of Fame. Some players can't handle that push, but I'm convinced it made him a better player." Lynn had a fine career spread over 17 seasons, but the numbers support Remy's claim: Lynn's best baseball came during his 6 full seasons in Boston.

But the city's attention to baseball can be inspirational—and intimidating. Some players and managers don't like the fact that each of the Red Sox's 162 games are held up and studied as if they are stones analyzed by a gemologist. The slightest cracks or imperfections can be debated for hours and, sometimes, years.

Two World Series titles and 22 years later, Boston still has an unsolved question from Game 6 of the 1986 Mets–Red Sox World Series: Did former manager John McNamara decide on his own to take his ace, Roger Clemens, out of the game with the season hanging in the balance? Or did Clemens, bothered by a blister, ask out after the seventh inning with his team ahead by one run? After Boston lost the memorable series in seven games and extended its championship famine to 68 years, McNamara sat in his office and stared at radio play-by-play man Joe Castiglione.

"Why me?" the manager finally said. "Why did this have to happen to me? I go to church every day. Why me?"

At least McNamara had a job to return to the next season. Little, who led Boston to Game 7 of the 2003 American League Championship Series, wasn't so fortunate.

With his refusal to make one eighth-inning call to the bullpen, Little unwittingly helped change modern baseball in Boston. The consequence of his decision to stay with a tiring Pedro Martinez was predictable: frothing fans in Boston wanted him gone and so did his bosses (some of whom were frothing, too).

There was an Old West feeling to New England in October 2003. Angry and frustrated Red Sox fans, with their title drought stretched to 85 years, played the mob. Little played the villain who needed to be out of town by sundown. The option year on his contract was not renewed, thus creating an opening in the office that, during baseball season, is more scrutinized than the governor's.

If anyone was taking bets back in November 2003, the smart money was that the new guy, Terry Francona, wouldn't make it in Boston. He didn't have a winning record as a big-league manager, he carried a handle, *players' manager*, that's an obscenity to the steak-and-potatoes sports fan, and he appeared to be too nice; one of the first things he did at his initial press conference was shout out his cell phone number to a large group of reporters.

Before Francona took the job, 32 different men had tried, unsuccessfully, to bring Boston just one championship in 85 years. Francona has done it twice in 4 years, using a formula that even a city as old as Boston has never seen.

CHAPTER 1

Blame the Manager

On the October night when most of New England directed its rage at Grady Little, Terry Francona was in suburban Philadelphia, halfway paying attention.

First he watched one of his three daughters play in a high school volleyball game. Then, grudgingly, he went home and tuned in to the final innings of the playoff series between the Boston Red Sox and New York Yankees. He certainly wasn't excited about spending his time looking at the Red Sox, so he increased the volume on his TV. That way he could travel from room to room and listen to the game when it became too frustrating to watch. He was the bench coach for the Oakland A's, the team the Red Sox had eliminated from the postseason, so it was hard to see Boston where he thought Oakland should have been. *I still think we're better than the Red Sox. Hell, we were up two games on them. If we had just run the bases a little better* . . . Talk about impact TV: at no point did he imagine that the broadcast was about to show him something that would land him a job in Boston.

The winning team on that night would represent the American League in the 2003 World Series. Through seven and a half innings at Yankee Stadium, the Red Sox appeared to be that team. They held a 5 to 2 lead, a cushion that would allow Little to leverage his bullpen and get the final five outs of the game. The Boston manager had his best pitcher, Pedro Martinez, on the mound. But Martinez was tired. He had allowed a one-out double to Derek Jeter in the eighth, and he clearly didn't have a reservoir of brilliant pitches remaining, at least not enough to get through the muscular Yankees lineup.

The way Little's bosses saw it, the manager had several favorable options among his relief pitchers. But John Henry, Larry Lucchino, and Theo Epstein, all men Little reported to, knew that the real issue wasn't solely about a bullpen that had given up just 2 runs in its previous 25 innings of work. The issue was that in need of five outs, Little was more likely to choose instinct over science. So as the Fox television cameras were focused on the drama before them on the field, few people realized that there was also a philosophical clash coming to a head at the same time.

It was Feel versus Numbers, Tradition versus Something New, Acoustic versus Electric, Jocks versus Geeks. And it had been simmering for two seasons. Little didn't believe that he had to apologize for his style. He was a friendly Southerner who was always ready with a story and a joke. He knew how to talk to players and tap into whatever it was that either motivated them or brought on insecurity. The numbers packets and various reports from the front office were all right, but if he had to make an in-game decision that was the difference between winning and losing, he was usually going to side with flesh and blood.

Henry, the principal owner of the Red Sox, wasn't nearly as emotional as Little. In fact, Henry became a billionaire by creating a mechanical trading system based on following trends. He believed that no one could predict the future in any industry, hedge funds or baseball, but that there were always data that could help one make informed choices. Little's homespun style was fine with him, but he would have liked it more if that style had come with more solid reasons for baseball decisions.

The two men were as different as their baseball backgrounds: whereas Little's vision was shaped by managing hundreds of personalities and 2,000 games in the minor league sticks, Henry was drawn to the sport as an owner, a fan, and a lover of computer-simulation games. He was so taken with the inventive formulas and original writings of Bill James, a true baseball outsider, that he hired him to work for the Red Sox.

Clash.

Eighth inning. The score was 5 to 3 after Bernie Williams singled home Jeter. There was still the bullpen option. Still one out. Still Feel versus Numbers. Several members of the Boston ownership group and baseball operations staff were nervous when Little jogged from the third-base dugout to talk with Martinez. If they had to pinpoint one reason he had been a good hire, they would choose what they called his "social intelligence." They knew he had a politician's gift for canvassing a room and a preacher's for bringing people together. Frankly, they weren't sure how much he was willing to apply what they deemed important.

They even had a meeting about him earlier in the season. The agenda: how to best manage the manager. The conclusion: allow him the flexibility, for the most part, to manage in that folksy style of his. It couldn't be all bad, could it? They were on their way to 95 wins and the playoffs, and the manager deserved some credit for that. But they had to let him know, emphatically, that certain things were required of a Red Sox manager. The list wasn't long, maybe two or three things, but the list was nonnegotiable.

The necessity of the meeting was a clue that the relationship was doomed. They had to tell him to consider all the available information and use some of it? That was trouble, long before October in New York.

Little would later explain that he felt he gave his team the best chance to win by placing the ball and season in the wiry right hand of Martinez. As he looked into Martinez's eyes, Little didn't just see a pitcher who on average gave up the fewest earned runs, 2.22, in the league and would one day be in the Baseball Hall of Fame; he also saw an artist. The Geeks were fine with that. Their point was that after Martinez threw over 100 pitches, he was indeed an artist—but the art was more paintball than Picasso. Martinez, with talent and competitiveness to burn, was dramatically easier to hit once his pitch count exceeded 100.

Take him out. It was the silent scream for every Red Sox employee sitting there anxiously in the Bronx. It had to be silent. Imagine the response if the cameras had captured Epstein, the general manager, and Henry yelling at their manager. The screaming in New England, though, was real. Elderly Boston fans howled because they believed that the 2003 Red Sox were their best chance at baseball bliss before death. Some people yelled because for a Bostonian, the only thing worse than losing is losing to the Yankees. Some people shouted in the name of common sense. They waved at their TVs—*Wake up, Grady!*—as if that would snap him out of it.

He obviously didn't hear or see them, and it wouldn't have made a difference if he had. He appeared to be fed up with his organization's obsession with numbers. It was their brainstorm, not his, that led to an experiment in spring training. They actually tried to begin the season without a closer, which is heresy for a true baseball man. The media tabbed it "closer by committee." The idea was that different pitchers could get the most important outs of the game, whether those outs needed to be gotten in the seventh, eighth, or ninth innings.

Sure, it sounded fine on paper. But in the real baseball world, it was an intellectual exercise that made it impossible for him to set up his bullpen, and for his pitchers—real people, not charts on a page—to know what the hell was going on. And while the numbers detailing Martinez's decline after 100-plus pitches had crossed his desk, he still allowed his ace to throw 130 pitches in a first-round start against the A's. Numbers? Forget the numbers. This was insubordination.

There was a brief conversation with Martinez on the mound and then a return to the dugout. When Little walked away with his hands in his jacket pockets, he essentially walked away from his job.

His successor alternately watched and listened in Pennsylvania. He made no assumptions or judgments. It wasn't his team, so he wasn't familiar with all the personalities. He knew a thing or two about the silver-haired Boston manager, but nothing that would give him any insight into what was happening on the field. Pro baseball is the land of a few degrees of separation, so wouldn't you know that Francona had played with Little's younger brother, Bryan—nicknamed "Twig"—in the minors? Or that Grady Little and Francona had been housemates for a couple months in 1992? It was the Arizona Fall League, where future big-leaguers, prospects and managers, congregate to sharpen their games. Little and Francona held two of the coaching spots for the Grand Canyon Rafters, with Little managing and Francona in place as his third-base coach. They lived in a Mesa condo and often shared the 30-minute commute to Grand Canyon University in Phoenix. They got along just fine, but it wasn't as if they spent hours trading baseball philosophies. What Francona remembered most about Little was that he was the pleasant man of routines who couldn't drive by any of the desert's 7-Elevens without stopping in and picking up some lottery tickets.

They were both a long way from the short-season anonymity

of Arizona now. Little was in a different kind of fall league, the national stage of the big-league playoffs, making managerial decisions under the Yankee Stadium lights. Francona had no idea what Little's challenges were in New York. Was someone hurt? Was someone scared? Did Little feel that he didn't have the matchups he wanted in the bullpen?

Once you've managed, you always remind yourself that there are dozens of factors of which fans are unaware. On that night, October 16, Francona was a lot like those fans. But when he actually stopped moving from room to room, he tried to think of all the options that both managers had. In other words, the A's bench coach was thinking in depth and weighing all of Boston's possibilities, and he wasn't invested in the team. He wasn't even sure he wanted to watch. He didn't know it at the time and neither did the Red Sox management, but he was exactly what they needed.

Eighth inning. A few seconds after Little's pep talk to Martinez, Hideki Matsui hit a ground-rule double to right field. There was still no call to the bullpen. Still one out. What was this? Before anyone could answer the rhetorical question, Jorge Posada was in mid-swing. It was a 2-2 pitch and the proud Martinez, as spent as he might have been, wasn't giving in. He had reached 93 miles per hour on one of his fastballs to Matsui. He got up to 95 on a fastball to Posada. On the 2-2 pitch, the plan for Martinez was to deliver a fastball in on the New York catcher's hands. The plan was successful in a sense because Posada was jammed.

"Pedro sawed him off," said Gabe Kapler, who was a Red Sox reserve outfielder. "But Posada kept his hands inside the ball, which is very tough to do in that situation." Posada didn't smash the baseball, but he didn't have to. He had enough strength to lift the ball to right-center field for a game-tying double. Kapler watched from the dugout and still insists, "I don't disagree with leaving Pedro in the game. I don't think any of the guys in the dugout were saying, 'Get him out of there.' He threw some great pitches in that inning."

Finally, with the score tied at 5, Martinez's night was over. Baseball is funny sometimes: Martinez's final pitch, his 123rd, was one of his best. But there were few people in the stadium willing to take a clinical view of that pitch, and the bosses weren't among them. Hadn't they warned the supervisor about the employee's performance in overtime? It had literally and figuratively become a new day. The game was going to be extended, which meant it would end in the early-morning hours of the 17th. The stadium crowd quickly grasped how out of place, and joyous, the moment was. This had already been a fierce series, America's version of a gritty European soccer rivalry. Less than a week earlier, in the third game, two Yankees fought with a part-time groundskeeper in the Fenway Park bullpen and were charged with assault and battery. Earlier in the same game, Martinez had aimed a pitch near the head of Karim Garcia, who was one of the bullpen fighters. The pitch eventually led to the benches clearing, and Martinez found himself playing matador to 72-year-old coach Don Zimmer's raging bull. The angry series, from the view of New Yorkers, had suddenly turned charitable. What a country: the richest team in baseball was getting a subsidy from the manager of the Red Sox. It was as if Little had randomly decided that he was going to pick up the tab for each of the 56,000 Yankee fans in the house.

If Little had mishandled the pitching in the eighth, what made anyone think he would find the deft touch in extra innings? The only thing that would bail him out, short- and long-term, was someone hitting a home run that would carry the Red Sox to the World Series. Yet the reality was that he was boxed in. Late-inning managing is a new version of gin rummy, a version in which the object is to hold onto your cards as long as possible before playing them at the perfect time. Not only was the man across from Little, Joe Torre, able to do that with his bullpen, he also saw that Little had misplayed his hand. In a three-run game, New York's Mariano Rivera was not a factor; in a tie game late, he was the most devastating pitching weapon either side had. Rivera had earned his reputation in games in which the stakes were highest. Simplicity was what made him great. He threw one pitch, a cut fastball, and he mastered it. It came out of his hand with no spin, meaning the seams of the baseball offered a batter no clue of what the ball was going to do next. From a batter's perspective, the ball would travel one distance for its first 60 feet. Then, in its final 6 inches, it would devour the barrel of the bat like a 93-mile-per-hour termite. Rivera was going to throw that predictable yet hard-to-hit pitch over and over. He knew it, and so did they.

The contrast was haunting for New England. It was the Boston manager's rejection of simplicity—the pitcher is tired, so take him out—that pushed him and his team away from potential greatness. Little truly was facing opponents in every corner: Rivera, who was rested and prepared to pitch until last call; Red Sox owners and members of the front office, most of them furious at the manager; Little's own strategic weaknesses, which cost him yet another late chance at tilting the bullpen in his favor; and Red Sox fans, who had already turned his name into one of the dirtiest regional profanities.

Of course, all of it was too much to overcome. New York won, 6 to 5. Rivera pitched three innings, one and a half more than usual, and allowed just two hits. The game ended in the 11th inning when Aaron Boone hit a home run off Tim Wakefield. The home run landed and, officially, Boston's nausea turned to anger. It was the type of anger that could be reconciled one day, but not until the Red Sox won a World Series. Who in New England was going to wait 'til next year with Little? The region's residents, religious about their baseball team, already wavered in their faith of the manager. Now they didn't trust him.

Little was gone. The players must have known it after the game when Little, in a quiet clubhouse, went to each of them and whispered thanks and encouragement. They knew it on the plane ride home, a 38-minute flight from New York to Boston, 38 minutes when no one spoke unless they were answering yes-or-no questions from flight attendants. *Sir, would you like a beer? Okay, you need something stronger?* Little's seat on the 767 was in first class. He was a few feet away from the men who would soon decide that they wouldn't pick up the option year on his contract. There really wasn't much for anyone to say—in the air.

By the time the team landed in Boston early on a Friday morning, the movement among the fans was already afoot. Grady had to go. He was the number-one topic of the weekend and the week that followed. He was dragged from forum to forum: newspapers, sports-talk radio, TV opinion shows, message boards, office cubicles, schools, churches, and, of all places, the *Rock the Vote* Democratic presidential debate on CNN. The *Boston Herald* even had a story outlining the ways Little's decision had cost the city at least $7 million. Boston would have hosted the first two World Series games, and in addition to the 800 hotel rooms major league baseball would have needed, there would have been a boost for local bars, restaurants, stores, buses, and cabs.

"Say hello to our little Grady," wrote *Herald* reporter Cosmo Macero Jr., "a one-man local recession."

No one wanted to talk about his fine winning percentage as a manager. Nor was there much space to discuss some of the strides he had made with the team off the field, strides that helped the clubhouse run smoothly. After all, the year before Little's arrival, the Red Sox were just as likely to be fodder for *Baseball*

Tonight as they were for Dr. Phil. The pre–Little Red Sox was a team that could be measured by games as well as episodes. They had it all: angry backup players as well as an often sour superstar in Nomar Garciaparra; an aloof superstar in Manny Ramirez as well as a gifted and temperamental starting pitcher in Martinez; a manager and general manager—Jimy Williams and Dan Duquette—who became adversaries, as well as an interim manager/substitute teacher—Joe Kerrigan—whom the players mocked and cursed; an ownership group that lacked vision and charisma; and a small, old ballpark with almost no room to think in peace. Little, Henry, Epstein, and Lucchino all arrived in 2002, and all were key figures in rebuilding the park and the relationships that went on inside it.

While the fans and front office had different views of how significant Little's presence in the clubhouse was—insignificant to the fans, extremely significant to the front office—ultimately both groups were going in the same direction: no more Grady. The good-bye was inevitable; the streets of Boston practically cried out for it.

Maybe Little would have been given the benefit of the doubt in a different part of the country. Some cities might have blamed Martinez for not finishing the job. Or they might have pointed to Wakefield for allowing the winning home run. In another time, say the 1960s and 1970s, fans wouldn't mention pitch counts and managers wouldn't be vilified for working an ace to exhaustion in the most important game of the year. In another place, the words of baseball author Bill Deane might have spoken for a majority. Defending Little's decision, Deane wrote, "Today's managers have learned that they rarely get second-guessed when they make a substitution, only when they don't, and they manage accordingly—not necessarily to win, but to avoid media scrutiny and justify their own existence."

Boston's fans didn't want to hear any of it. Little hadn't just embarrassed them, he'd embarrassed them in front of New York. The people hadn't seen a baseball champion in 85 years, and in their opinion, Little was a roadblock to progress. His severance package was a pile of cash and 85 years' worth of fury.

When Francona heard about Boston's Little backlash, he shook his head.

"Man," he said. "That place sounds crazy."

He was right, and the crazy place was about to become his home.

CHAPTER 2

The Test

It didn't take Terry Francona long to get his introduction to insider Boston. What seemed strange to him at the time was that the introduction didn't actually happen there. He was in another city of the powerful and connected, Washington, D.C., when he was plainly told what the decision-makers at Fenway Park were thinking.

It was three days after what was being called "The Grady Game," and Francona was on the road with his son, Nick. Part of the family's scouting report on Nick was that he was a bright kid who was a born negotiator. He may have been a senior pitcher at the Lawrenceville School in New Jersey, but Nick wasn't looking for baseball to be the centerpiece of his collegiate career. He was searching for a school that could best help him get to the field of his true passion: high-level financial management. Georgetown was one of the schools that interested him, so father and son spent time on campus and socialized with other parents and prospective students.

At one point on their tour, they found themselves in a room filled with about 100 people, a mass of handshakes, nametags, and nice-to-meet-yous. As they talked with each other, they noticed a man working his way through the crowd and coming toward them.

"Terry Francona," he said with a knowing smile. "You're going to be the next manager of the Boston Red Sox."

The man introduced himself, but Francona had seen dozens of people that day. The name of this enthusiastic Red Sox fan blended in with everyone else he had met. He didn't know that the fan, Mike Barnicle, was a longtime Boston columnist and multimedia personality. He also didn't realize the power and reach of a Boston whisper. The city is too small and too chatty for institutions to hold on to secrets, and the Red Sox are one of the most important institutions in town.

As far as Francona knew, the Red Sox had a manager, yet here was someone saying that the job would be his. He hadn't received a single call or message from New England, so this was obviously someone who didn't know what he was talking about. Francona would figure it out eventually, but that day on the Georgetown campus, Barnicle knew more about his future than he did.

Francona's view of his options was fairly simple. He wanted to manage again, as he had for four losing seasons with the Philadelphia Phillies, but it wouldn't be awful if his best option was returning to Oakland. There were a lot of things about the organization he liked, including the way the A's tried to work around money, their biggest obstacle. Other than wins and smarts, everything the A's had was a fraction compared to the colossal Red Sox and Yankees: attendance, payroll, and regional sports-network cash.

The concept of getting more out of less fascinated Francona, and when he wasn't listening to general manager Billy Beane's ideas about baseball, he was teasing him about his fame. For weeks, Francona made sure he was close to *Moneyball,* the Michael Lewis book that made Beane a national celebrity. As soon as Beane would walk onto team buses and planes, an already seated Francona would be near an entrance, greeting him by reading loudly from passages about Beane's charm and intelligence. Jokes aside, he thought a lot of the ideas made sense. He also believed that an over-reliance on anything, numbers or hunches, was foolish. He had some good arguments with Beane's Harvard-trained assistant, Paul DePodesta, a smart executive who had never played in the majors. "You know what, Paul? If you take my point of view and your point of view, and we just met in the middle, we'd have a chance to have an unbelievable organization." It sounded simple, but he knew the Ivy Leaguers in baseball were sometimes too smart to listen to the common sense of the jocks, and the jocks were sometimes too stubborn to listen to the intellectual Ivy Leaguers. Francona was willing to question and debate any aspect of baseball, so his curiosity about the game and devotion to it were embraced by the A's.

It also helped that his buddy Ken Macha was the manager. They were both from western Pennsylvania, so they understood the same language; it was the local tongue of *warshing* clothes and shopping *dontahn*, a rugged brand of English that sounded like it was made in the mills that also produced the steel. It was an accent that Roberta Francona—"Birdie" to all her friends—had drilled out of her only son, Terry, so much so that by the time he worked with Pittsburgh native Macha, Francona spoke in a purposeful style that made it seem as if he were checking over each word before releasing it to the world.

Anyway, he could have dinner with Macha, laugh with him, analyze each night's matchups for him, and give him a different perspective during games. Macha had insisted on holding the job for him on his first staff, even when Francona suggested that the position might be better for someone else. Macha would hear none of it. He didn't give in until Francona committed to be on his 2003 coaching staff.

The A's were a fun group of guys and a good team, so Francona
enjoyed himself. But it wasn't the mental and physical grind of
managing, a grind that he knew and missed. There were times,
especially after tough losses, when Francona would pass Macha's
office and recognize that not-enough-sleep managerial haze.

"I'm going to head home to sleep, Macha," he'd say on his way
out. "And I know you're not."

He knew the job was demanding, and he wanted back in. In
Philadelphia, with a night game followed by one the next afternoon, he'd sleep on the floor in his Veterans Stadium office rather
than make the 30-mile drive home. He'd blast the air conditioning,
wrap himself in a flimsy sheet, and collapse on a blow-up mattress.
He'd instruct his friend Frank Coppenbarger to wake him up as
soon as he arrived in the clubhouse at 7:00 A.M. Coppenbarger, the
Phillies' director of team travel and equipment, always knew what
to expect at 7:00 when he opened the door to that cold, dark re-
frigerator that Francona called an office.

"He'd have junk food everywhere," Coppenbarger recalls.
"There would be Reese's peanut butter cup wrappers, empty bags
of chips, and grape stems all over the place. And he'd wake up
shivering because he'd have the AC up so high."

He wasn't planning to repeat all aspects of Philadelphia. He was
just 37 years old when the Phillies hired him after the 1996 season,
and they didn't hire him to win. They didn't quite phrase it that
way, but everyone who was paying attention got it. The team had
reached the World Series in 1993, and now it was rebuilding.
"They'd finally figured out they weren't going to be able to build
anything around the leftovers from the '93 team," says Jayson
Stark, a former *Philadelphia Inquirer* baseball reporter who now
works with ESPN. "So they essentially announced, 'We're starting
over.' And that meant the manager wasn't there to try to win

anything. He was there to try to build something. . . . But Terry's bullpen was so bad, and his complementary parts were so mediocre, that there was no way the manager was ever going to look like [Hall of Fame manager] John McGraw." Francona was along for the ride, a kid manager charged with raising big-league kids—even if his profile was similar to theirs: young guy trying to make it. And that included things beyond baseball.

Just two years earlier, when he was managing in the minor leagues, he and wife Jacque's bank account dwindled until it rested on a number that was never meant to live alone: zero. He earned a $32,000 salary in his final season as the leader of the Double-A Birmingham Barons. Jacque had a job, too, working part-time as a visiting nurse. All six of the Franconas were there in Alabama—Terry, Jacque, Nick, Alyssa, Leah, and Jamie—happy and living paycheck to paycheck. They were a baseball family, and at least they had work in the industry. They had themselves a Chevy Astro van, they had a townhouse in Arizona, and they were having fun. They'd be just fine.

When Francona was closing in on the Phillies job, a man who would become one of his best friends, Bill Giles, learned of his financial situation. Giles, the team's chairman and president, floated the young manager a $50,000 loan to help purchase a house in suburban Yardley. There was no timetable on repaying the loan. He just wanted the rookie manager to have a clear head in his new city and to have affection for it. Liking the city was not a problem for Francona. Putting together more wins than losses, unfortunately, was another story.

Shortly after Francona's single season in Oakland ended with the playoff loss to Boston, he went on a couple interviews for manager's jobs. He had one of those classic dating-nightmare interviews in Baltimore: after 5 minutes it's clear that you don't want them and they don't want you, so the dominant thought at the table becomes, "Exit strategy." He knew things weren't going to go well when, right off the top, he was asked how he felt about bringing back the entire coaching staff. He replied by saying that it didn't sound like Orioles management was truly interested in changing the team's culture.

Clearly, not a good fit. The Orioles hired Lee Mazzilli instead.

He had an interview in Chicago with Ken Williams, the general manager of the White Sox. They had known each other for years, so there wouldn't be a need for any of those awkward icebreakers. They met at a restaurant near O'Hare International Airport, where the conversation wasn't close to the one Francona had imagined. The interview was disjointed and full of interruptions. If it wasn't the waiter checking in to see if the men had everything they needed, it was Williams splitting and buttering a roll just as Francona was making what he thought was a key point.

No hard feelings. When you're interviewed at a restaurant near the airport, you're probably not the top candidate anyway. The White Sox decided to go with Ozzie Guillen.

Boston? Well, Francona had a couple of conversations about Boston with Bud Black, one of his former teammates. The rumors were that Black, not Francona, was the man the Red Sox were targeting to replace the officially dismissed Grady Little. Black, the pitching coach for the Angels, wasn't sure if he wanted to manage on the East Coast. He had already had some lengthy conversations with the Red Sox about the job, although he hadn't formally interviewed. He called Francona for advice, and Francona tried to persuade him to do it.

"Look at it this way, Blackie: Boston is a good job and you know you'll have a pretty good team. If you don't like it, you can do something else after a couple years. It's a great opportunity."

It wasn't long after that conversation—it seemed like a few hours—that Francona got word that Boston wanted to talk with him about managing the team. It was the first time since D.C. that he had heard his name in a Red Sox sentence. Maybe that fan on the Georgetown campus had been on to something after all.

After the phone call from Boston, it was Francona's turn to reach out to Black.

"Blackie, I have to tell you that I'm a little embarrassed. I was talking to you about what you should do in Boston, and they just called me to interview for the job."

Hearing those words from his friend made Black's decision easier. He had been going back and forth on whether it was the right time and place for him to manage. Knowing that a friend of his was also in the mix—Francona was convinced the job was Black's if he wanted it—meant that it was time to step back. He withdrew his name from consideration. With Black deciding to stay in Los Angeles, Boston's finalists were Francona; Dodgers third-base coach Glenn Hoffman, a former Red Sox shortstop; Angels bench coach Joe Maddon; and Rangers first-base coach DeMarlo Hale, a former Red Sox minor league manager.

Inside Fenway Park, coming up with that list had led to some considerable hand-wringing. The fans celebrated because they didn't have to see Little anymore, but they also didn't have to hire the next guy. As crazy as the thought might have been to the fans, finding Little's replacement wasn't going to be easy. His strengths and weaknesses had both been obvious, which made dealing with him simpler. He didn't always listen to his bosses, but at least they didn't have to cast about trying to diagnose his issues. They knew all his tendencies, and he knew theirs. Now they were on to the unknown.

Since there was such urgency to move Little out of town, many

New Englanders glossed over the fact that Theo Epstein, the Red Sox general manager, was going to be making his first managerial hire. Epstein was 28 years old when he was named GM in November 2002, making him the youngest man in baseball history with that title. Right around the time of his one-year anniversary on the job, Epstein began searching for a manager capable of leading the Red Sox to the World Series and actually winning it. It would have been a hilarious assignment if it hadn't been his. What did he know about finding a manager?

Before his career took him to Boston, he had worked in San Diego. It seemed that Padres manager Bruce Bochy never so much as twitched in that seat as Epstein arrived in Southern California in 1995, worked in baseball operations, went to law school at night, scouted, and, 7 years later, boarded a flight to Boston to become assistant GM of his hometown Red Sox.

Funny, but Epstein had been on more rigorous GM hunts than managerial ones. In his last days as an assistant GM, he had recommended Oakland's Beane for the opening in Boston. Beane agreed to a Boston contract and was on his way to working for an organization where *Moneyball* would take on new meaning for him. The Red Sox were so bankrolled that they could afford to pay for expensive players and pay off expensive mistakes. If spending money was the question, the answer was usually, "Yes, of course." But Beane had doubts about leaving the Bay Area, and those doubts led to a professional U-turn back to Oakland. That's when history and the Red Sox called for Epstein.

Epstein's age wasn't the only thing that made him a notable GM. Nor was it bloodlines that allowed him to say that his grandfather, a *Casablanca* screenwriter, created some of the greatest one-liners—*Here's looking at you, kid*—in the history of American cinema. And although his good looks and savvy once had him on New England's list of dream bachelors, just after Patriots quarterback Tom Brady, being tall and handsome had nothing to do with sound decision-making. What made Epstein stand out was his balance, a balance that gave him permission to connect with multiple camps and have credibility in all of them.

He wasn't all spreadsheet or all scout; he was a little of both. He could hang out with the suits and talk their corporate talk, and he could strum a guitar while admiring the poetry of Pearl Jam. He had a need to examine a situation from all sides, a routine thoroughness that protected him from being a reactionary. No one was as hot-tempered and miserable to be around as he following a loss, but he was smart enough to avoid all decisions while his misery was fresh. It was a good quality for any executive to have, and a requirement for the GM of the Red Sox.

Really, it was a job of being constantly seduced and lobbied. Everyone in the region had an internal No Championship calendar. Each time the pages flipped from yet another barren year—'86, '87, '88, '89 . . . —the tension increased. People became more cynical and desperate. Implausible trades became plausible. Irrational signings became rational. The word "future" became an occasional f-bomb.

The GM was always having his shoulder tapped, his jacket pulled, his ear whispered into. Epstein understood it because he had done it and grown up around it. He knew the agenda-setting impact of the sports columnists and sports-talk radio hosts. They were eloquent, sure, but they were selling eloquent frustration, and it all amounted to an immediate call to action. They wrote and spoke to an opinionated and hungry audience, an audience that spanned, at least, the six New England states.

Sometimes the people wanted management to do something big and do it now; sometimes they saw a promising prospect, considered him the next great thing, and were willing to walk with him to the altar. They flashed anger, but they still wore badges of family honor, and those badges covered the heartbeats of romantics. It always came back to a desire to win just once for Grandpa or Nana or old Uncle Roscoe. It was easy for any executive, no matter how brilliant, to be lured into their emotional dance.

One of the first things Epstein promised himself in November 2003 was that he wouldn't be pressured to go after a so-called big name to replace Little. Even the men recognized as the best managers in the game, Bobby Cox and Mike Scioscia, might find trap doors in Boston that they hadn't thought of in Atlanta and Los Angeles. That logic was reversible, too: a candidate might have had trouble with a team in another market, but that didn't mean the same man wouldn't be able to thrive in Boston.

Epstein began making phone calls to find out about Francona, and Francona did the same thing to get a glimpse of Epstein. A few times, they would have been better off doing a three-way conference call. They knew some of the same people and had some of the same sources. One of their mutual friends, Cleveland GM Mark Shapiro, kept it simple when Francona asked about Epstein.

"Don't bullshit this guy," Shapiro warned. "He's too smart to fall for it. He'll tie you up in knots."

Those words sounded good to Francona. The concept of fooling someone to get a job never crossed his mind. His energy was spent writing and studying. He filled nine pages with notes on how he felt about pro baseball and managing, knowing that if he wrote his thoughts he'd be able to verbalize them. He wrote how important it was for players to show respect for the game simply by being on time, and he wrote about observing players. He wrote that you can peek into the soul of a player early in the morning during spring training, when few people are watching on the back fields; that's when the players who have passion stand out from the indifferent pack. When he was finished writing, he picked up a Red Sox media guide and committed every face he saw to memory. Anyone could recognize all the people from TV, but he wanted to put names with the assortment of unfamiliar faces. It didn't matter if the employee worked in scouting, public relations, or the clubhouse—if there was a picture in the guide, Francona was going to learn that person's name.

Epstein, meanwhile, was trying to figure out how to structure a relevant interview. He knew he didn't want it to be a traditional question-and-answer session. Francona would be sitting there in a jacket and tie, which in itself was far from reality; this was the same man who once told the Phillies that the most important rule of the dress code was that no one was allowed to look worse than he did. And he was the one known for leaving his sport coats in wrinkled heaps on the floor. Epstein didn't care if Francona's pocket squares were coordinated with his ties. He wanted to see how his mind worked and how he reacted to pressure. His plan was to combine the best elements of the standard interview with an experimental technique designed to simulate the intensity of the dugout.

There would be no business travelers, waiters, or buttered rolls to distract them when they met at Fenway in November 2003. One of Epstein's assistant general managers at the time, Josh Byrnes, joined them for what was going to be a full shift of talking baseball.

It was obvious to Francona that these two had done their homework, and their preparation relaxed him. They had talked to enough people to at least get a silhouette of his years in Philadelphia, so when they mentioned specific things it felt more like a conversation than an interrogation. They knew that he had taken his share of hits on talk radio, with hosts and callers labeling him Fran*coma*. The fans there didn't like the way he rested players on day games following night games—*Stop babying these guys, you idiot*—and they had endless laughs at his expense when he didn't play Scott Rolen—on Scott Rolen Bobblehead Day.

He didn't mind telling Epstein and Byrnes that he had planned to give Rolen that day off long before he had been aware of the promotion. Rolen needed it, and the third baseman was appreciative when the manager didn't change his mind just because humans and figurines were shaking their heads at him.

The rap on him was that he was too nice, and he didn't entirely disagree. He didn't have the jackass gene and he didn't pretend that he did. He admitted to Epstein that there were times when he had been too protective of his players, but he also didn't believe in communicating with them through the media. He was similar to Epstein in that he'd wait a beat to make sure his emotions didn't lead him to overreaction with a player or coach. Then, on a plane or bus ride or standing on the edge of the outfield grass the next day, he'd say what he needed to. If the choices were talking tough to impress reporters and fans or working privately to make sure players were accountable to both him and their teammates, he would always choose the latter.

Of course, that philosophy leads to assumptions: if no one outside the clubhouse sees it happen or hears it happen, they assume that it doesn't happen. The Red Sox, though, searched deeper. They already knew about a story from late in the 2000 season, Francona's last in Philadelphia, when the manager tried to send outfielder Bobby Abreu home for the year. He liked Abreu, but he was frustrated with his play and attitude. He knew that if he saw the issues, everyone else on the team did as well. Francona explained to GM Ed Wade that not sending Abreu home would undermine the manager in the clubhouse. Wade nixed the plan anyway. Francona knew at that moment that he was going to be fired at the end of the season.

He didn't regret getting along exceptionally well with Curt Schilling, Doug Glanville, Rico Brogna, and Rolen. He played poker and golf with Giles and hung out with him in the Poconos. His family and Coppenbarger's shared Thanksgiving dinner. In a nutshell, he was a hard worker who also enjoyed having fun and talking to everybody. That might be a good thing for managers in the American workforce, but in professional sports the freaks are the managers and coaches who dare to be well adjusted.

Epstein was intrigued by the bald man in glasses. He wanted to have a baseball conversation with even more weight, so he handed Francona a pen and a multiple-choice test. All 16 questions were geared toward finding out how a manager ranked his priorities in several categories.

"Take your time filling it out," Epstein said as Francona went to work. "There's no right answer."

No right answer. That was rich. It was a 20-minute head trip and Francona loved it. Okay, so they were trying to see where all the puzzle pieces—relationships with players, relationships with the media, handling the pitching staff—were slotted in his world. He didn't mind. He even chuckled to himself when he glanced at one of the potential answers to the question, "What's most important to you?" Potential answer: "(D) Making sure your uniform looks good in the dugout." If they hired him, they would rarely see his uniform because it was usually covered with a fleece jacket. He didn't care how he looked. He was just eager to share his thoughts and be in a position to get a second chance.

He finished the test in front of Epstein and Byrnes, his two relaxed proctors. They had been telling the truth when they said there was no right answer, but they hadn't been completely honest. What they left out was that all the answers could be right, but there was a wrong way to defend those answers when questioned about them. They didn't want anyone who would wilt from his opinions or have opinions with no process to them. Epstein believed he'd get more out of a conversation about baserunning, defense, and pitching if he knew how Francona prioritized those things.

It was half test, half talking point. Epstein quickly noticed that Francona had some law school in his answers, not in terms of being legalistic, but in the way his responses were layered. He seemed to consider, naturally and thoroughly, a handful of possibilities before making a decision, and the decision itself was delivered in a few seconds. After a while, it was an interview in name only. It had become a skull session, and it was so fun that they had barely noticed that 1:00 had become 3:00 in a blink. And that was before the true test, the one that would cause beads of sweat to form on Francona's head.

They had all moved into a Fenway suite with a flat-screen TV already in place. Francona sat on a brown leather couch, and Epstein and Byrnes handed him a partial line score from an A's–Angels game. They explained that they wanted to see him in action. Talking about baseball was fun and all, but they really wanted to see how he applied all those sensible principles of his. Anyone could have a great day interviewing, right? How would he respond when they turned on the TV in this wood-paneled room and dropped him in the middle of the seventh inning?

Francona knew about games that seemed to have their own V-8 engines, games that moved ten times as fast in the dugout as they appeared to in the seats or in the press box. On nights like those in Philadelphia, he'd look at his longtime baseball brother, Brad Mills, and say, "Stay with me, Millsie." But Millsie wasn't in that Fenway suite. It was Francona and that game, a Lamborghini that wanted to drive itself. It was the dirtiest trick to play on a manager who cares about preparation: asking him to make decisions in someone else's game without the benefit of that person's information.

Epstein put the DVD on pause and set the scene: "It's the seventh inning, you're managing Oakland, and Barry Zito is on the mound. He has thrown one hundred and five pitches, and here's your chart of who's available in the bullpen. Here's who the other team has coming up. Here's where you are in the season . . ." He pushed PLAY and said, "You have two minutes."

Once again, that sport coat was in a heap somewhere. The tie was loosened. The sweat spread. Streams of information tumbled out of him: "I see this head-to-head matchup but I don't put too much weight into it because that was from a couple years ago . . . This left-right split is pretty consistent, so I'm going to rely on that . . . I see on the bullpen chart that my guy has been used three days in a row, so I'm not going to use him even though we need to win this game—he can't pitch four days in a row."

He was involved in this simulation now. Rocking, cursing, sweating. It wasn't his game, but he knew things about all these players. Even though he felt like he was sinking at times, he was making an impression because he seemed to have a dossier on everyone at his fingertips. He made Epstein and Byrnes laugh at one point when he worked his way through the seventh and eighth innings, with designs on giving the ball to Oakland closer Keith Foulke. But when Epstein pushed PLAY, Foulke was nowhere to be found. "Well," Francona deadpanned, "I always knew Macha was a dumbass."

It was a good line, but it wasn't the real story. The truth was that the interviewers had picked a game in which Foulke wasn't with the team. Still, Francona had made a point regarding a closer. He thought having one was essential for a manager. He told his interviewers that he agreed that crucial outs existed in the seventh and eighth innings, too, but a closer was the light that a manager worked his way toward during the game.

"By the way," he said, wiping away sweat, "we've talked a lot about preparation today, but I want you guys to know that I wouldn't manage like this. This isn't managing. I would have already known some of this stuff."

They looked at the clock and it was close to 6:00. They had spent an entire day together, talking, debating, and watching baseball. It was time for them to leave the park and head to a restaurant called the Atlantic Fish Company; they couldn't bring Francona to Boston without giving him some seafood. There were no tests with the menu, no tests on how he held his fork or sat in his chair. He ate, he laughed, and he had a few beers.

He remembered the time he and Millsie were driving in Arizona before a Phillies–Diamondbacks game. The Phillies stunk and the Diamondbacks didn't. He looked at Millsie, his friend since college, and said, "Imagine what it's like to be them, coming to the ballpark every night knowing that you have a chance to win."

God, he missed that. As he sat there having a beer, he knew Boston would be the type of place where he would have a chance every night. He wanted the job, and Epstein wanted him to have it. They agreed that if they were going to work together, they would need the type of relationship where one man didn't feel the need to tiptoe around the other.

"I don't need the manager to make decisions that I agree with, but I have the right to know why something happened—and vice versa," Epstein said to Francona. "And if we can't get to that point in our relationship, then I think we will fail."

Francona was relieved. He saw it the same way, so they shook on it.

New School

No one knows when it happened exactly. It's one of those cultural shifts that make it seem as if the world changes overnight: one day you're insensitive and inappropriate, and the next you're a comic with your own HBO special. Or you go to bed as a veteran senior analyst and wake up as the old guy who is forced to take the corporate buyout. Maybe you were the one "telling it like it is" before the curtain fell, and when it was raised again all your lines called for less vinegar and more diplomacy.

One night baseball drew the shades, and at daybreak an old job description—manager—had a brand-new glossary. And a handful of management styles went on the same list as the dodo.

It's not that Earl Weaver, Walter Alston, Dick Williams, and Sparky Anderson couldn't have handled the strategy of today. They're all in the Hall of Fame; the strategy of baseball Now would be a breeze to the men of baseball Then. Weaver was celebrating on-base percentages, obsessing over matchups, and despising bunts in Baltimore at least 30 years before those were principles in Oakland. Alston was one of the early arrivals on the first floor of social and athletic adaptation: in 1946, he was the

minor league manager of African Americans Roy Campanella
and Don Newcombe, a year before the Dodgers integrated the
sport; and in 1971, his Dodgers were among the first teams to
scrap the four-man pitching rotation in favor of the now-modern
five-man staff. They'd all figure out the baseball. It's the language
that would drive them crazy.

What, exactly, is "creating an atmosphere in which a player is
comfortable"? Why does a player hitting .233 need an "explanation" for why he's not in the lineup tonight? What's this drivel in
the newspaper about "showing up a player" by calling him out
within earshot of teammates, fans, and media? Alston was a lamb
compared to the late Billy Martin, but even he challenged his players to fights and followed them to their hotel rooms when they
came in past curfew. Do that now and you're taken through a media assembly line: The writers will throw their ink on you, they'll
pass you off to be yelled at on talk radio, they'll kick you into the
land of TV debates and 24-hour "Breaking News" crawls, and
they'll let you come to in a room where you can watch the original
incident online because a fan put it on YouTube.

Then there's the matter of your team. That is, you wouldn't
have one. This is the culture of comfort, so much so that even con-
frontations have to be handled with peace in mind. It's neither
good nor bad; it just is. A manager who cannot adjust to "building
good relationships" with players and overseeing an environment in
which "players hold each other accountable and police themselves"
will not make it. He can't. The game has too many powerful ten-
tacles attached to it: agents, lengthy and lucrative player contracts,
and a multibillion-dollar television deal that spans free TV as well
as cable. This is no kind of town for a counterculture sheriff.

"There's no way in hell I could manage in today's game," says
the 78-year-old Williams. "The players are making so much

money today that they're the ones calling the shots." It probably seems that way to Williams because he's from the school of mis-named "managers"; he didn't manage as much as he directed. He wasn't an imposing man, or at least the stat sheet said he wasn't supposed to be. He stood 6 feet tall and weighed 175 pounds. It didn't matter. He was demanding when he was talking baseball; if the subject was anything else and Williams had been drinking, players learned to avert their eyes when he walked toward the back of the plane. He could be scary.

As a player, Williams spent the final two seasons of his career as a utility man with the Red Sox. Three years later, in 1967, he be-came the 37-year-old manager in Boston. In between, he managed the Red Sox's Triple-A team in Toronto. In his ironically titled memoir, *No More Mr. Nice Guy*, he recalled how he came to be known as a managerial fighter while in Canada. One of his play-ers, Mickey Sinks, asked Williams if he thought the pitcher de-served to be called to the big leagues at the end of the season. Williams answered no; Sinks answered with a fist to the manager's right eye. Predictably, a scuffle ensued and the men wrestled until a trainer heard the commotion in Williams's office and broke up the fight.

"Apparently, I'd strained so much while bear-hugging Mickey Sinks that I'd shit my pants," Williams wrote. "Ruined that $49.95 seersucker suit . . . I called a clubhouse meeting the next day and brought out the pants. Let them see where I strained. Let them smell the stench. I told them: 'You mess with me, I'll shit all over you.' Then when they finished laughing, I added: 'If this is what it takes to win, everybody in this room will be wearing diapers.' They didn't laugh then."

In 1967, Williams was given a three-year contract to manage the Red Sox. His baseball and his Boston were less complicated then. There was media interest in the team, but it was nothing like the 135-person horde that covers each Red Sox game today. Williams joked that he had "four writers covering us—two for me and two against me." Curt Flood hadn't yet challenged baseball's reserve clause in court, so players were still a decade away from free agency. Under those rules, neither the players nor their union were powerful enough to prevent Williams or any other manager from ruling with a heavy touch. That's not to say that all successful managers of the era were similar to Williams. Red Schoendienst, the manager of Williams's hometown team, the St. Louis Cardinals, was as cool as Williams was intense. The difference, then, was that he wasn't required to be. If you had strong personal relationships with players, it was more choice than job requirement.

Williams couldn't wait to get his hands on the 1967 Red Sox. They had finished 9th in the 10-team American League in 1966. They averaged 10,000 fans per game. And Williams, of course, thought they were soft.

"It was a country club," he says from his Las Vegas–area home. "I tried to change the whole complexion of what that team was about."

He started by stripping the captaincy away from future Hall of Famer Carl Yastrzemski. It was nothing personal toward Yaz. The manager didn't think a ninth-place team needed to have a captain, plus he didn't believe that his talented left fielder had the makeup to be a vocal leader. Williams told general manager Dick O'Connell what he had in mind and went from there. He explained his thinking in his memoir:

Everyone wanted to know how I would break the news to owner Tom Yawkey's favorite player. What would I tell the legend? Hey, I didn't tell him squat. I recognized no captains, so I had no reason to speak to him as a captain. I told O'Connell there would be no captains, and that was that.

The Red Sox didn't have a lot of love for Williams, but they played well for him. His team went from ninth to first, winning the pennant on the final day of the regular season. They lost the World Series to the Cardinals in seven games. That team, with Triple Crown winner Yaz and Cy Young winner Jim Lonborg, was credited with more than a great ride. It's the team that regenerated Boston's dilapidated baseball spirit. It's the team that spawned a generation of Fenway preservationists; they so believe in the magic of the 96--year-old park that they'd rather suffer through the wrong-way seats and poor sight lines than start over with something new.

Unfortunately for the men who followed Williams, who was fired in September 1969, the 1967 team was the last New England would simply thank for the journey. The region had seen too much, come too close, and been empty-handed too long to say thanks for baseball seasons that produced no championships. The 1967 team got a pass because it was a generation's first love. Just over 10 years later, that innocent generation of lovers was introduced to bitterness and couples counseling. They didn't praise Don Zimmer's Red Sox for 99 wins and making it all the way to a one-game playoff against the Yankees; they immortalized their pain with an angry acknowledgment of the player who beat them: Bucky (Bleeping) Dent.

Williams had gotten his championships years earlier, managing the Oakland A's to two of their three consecutive titles in the early 1970s. In 1975, while managing the Angels, Williams made a point to introduce himself to Jerry Remy, his 22-year-old second baseman. Remy was a long way from home, a New Englander from Somerset, Massachusetts, playing for a man he feared. It was a nice spring day in California, and Remy was making his major league debut against the Kansas City Royals. His first big-league hit was an RBI single off Steve Busby, and he stood at first base feeling good about what he'd done.

Well, back to that introduction: Busby picked Remy off first.

"Hey," Williams barked at Remy. "Sit your ass down! If that ever happens again, your ass will be back in Salt Lake City so fast you won't know what hit you."

Remy sat and listened. Williams's plan, admittedly, was to either motivate through fear or to create an unlovable villain—himself—whom players hated so much that they actually played hard for him. Initially, he was able to hold Remy's attention by threatening to send him back to the minors in Utah. Later, after the manager developed some confidence in the kid, he gave him permission to steal bases on his own. That worked well until the day Remy was caught stealing and ran the Angels out of an inning.

"You're off your own," Williams announced.

He didn't speak to Remy for two weeks. Then one day after batting practice, Williams let it be known that they were talking again and that the second baseman was back on his own. "Did you learn your lesson?" he asked, knowing that an answer was unnecessary. The manager set the rules, and if you were a young player looking uphill at service time, you didn't question it.

That's the way it was when you played for Williams, Martin, Zimmer, and Gene Mauch. Those guys always seemed to outnumber the managers of the era whom the players were able to overthrow. The Washington Senators did have their "Underminers' Club," which they put together in hopes of running their manager, Red Sox icon Ted Williams, out of town. The Senators were so bad that no one knew the difference between their attempts to sabotage and their attempts to play baseball. The plan worked a bit too well: Teddy Ballgame was gone to Texas—along with the franchise, which moved there.

By the time Remy was traded to the Red Sox after the 1977 season, the phenomenon of free agency was in place. So was Zimmer, a hydrant of a man dually nicknamed "Popeye" and "The Gerbil" because of his bulging cheeks. The players may have been on the verge of a financial revolution, but that didn't mean Zimmer was going to be run over by them. In fact, that was the story around the majors. The game was going to have to dictate what happened to the feisty manager, because those men had no plans to change their personalities. They were going to keep doing what they did until evolution and/or losses spun them out of the dugout.

Remy remembers arriving at Fenway for a game and learning that he wasn't in the lineup. He had been struggling against lefties, but he had still expected to play. His disappointment was obvious, because he was told to "go talk to Zim."

"I hadn't walked two feet into his office before he lit into me," Remy says with a laugh. "He said, 'You want to know why you're not playing today? Because you suck against lefties, that's why.' And he said some other things, using 'Zim language' the whole time."

Zim may have used Zim language, but he was letting other voices creep into his head, especially in 1978, when the Red Sox held a 14½-game lead over the Yankees in mid-July and let the lead slip away. Baseball was changing and so was the sports atmosphere, so when Zim left the ballpark he wouldn't listen to music on his radio or 8-track tape player. He and his wife, Soot, would tune into WITS, the team's flagship radio station. The host, Glenn Ordway, had a call-in talk show from 8:00 P.M. until midnight. After games, Ordway and his callers would question some of the manager's choices.

Those questions usually had something to do with the daily decision to leave an injured-and-playing-like-it Butch Hobson at third base. Hobson had bone spurs in his right elbow, and he could be seen shaking his arm into place on the field. At the plate, he would literally adjust the loose bodies in his elbow until he found a position that he liked. Then he would lock in and try to hit a baseball. It wasn't a surprise when he committed a staggering 43 errors in 1978, while his fielding percentage of .899 was well below the league average of .954. He could get to the ball, but he couldn't throw it cleanly, often botching what should have been ordinary plays. Ordway and the fans called for backup Jack Brohamer to play. The more they pleaded, the more Zim dug in, and the more Hobson continued to play and short-arm those throws.

Zim was the manager of the team. He clearly knew things about the game and his players that no fan or member of the media could. Yet he couldn't pull himself away from the radio, a medium that he gave power by refusing to dismiss it. It was a routine: he and Soot would put on WITS, wince with the jabs, and Zim would confront Ordway the next day.

"He hates Ordway to this day," Remy says. "It's human nature: people can say whatever they want, but nobody enjoys getting ripped."

If managers weren't going to adjust to the players who played for them, they would have to make space for the writers and talkers who didn't. The talkers would call them idiots when certain players would just think it. The writers would call for their jobs when the players could only dream of it. Yes, the media were changing, too. In the old days, a lot of the writers had been unpaid team hands. They traveled with the players, ate with them, boozed with them, played cards with them, got enough scoops to satisfy the bosses, and turned their heads just at the right time so they could say, "I didn't see it" in good conscience. They knew all the secrets and kept most of them out of the paper. Everyone was happy.

But a couple of things got in the way—journalism and innovation—just as the toy department was about to get a new shipment of fluff and games. Some of the young journalists decided that they were going to be more than the paper's guilty pleasure. They weren't going to safely fill space in order to maintain ballpark status quo; they were becoming influential stars themselves, especially in New England. The renewed interest in the 1967 Red Sox had coincided with the rise of Tom Winship, a *Boston Globe* editor who preferred flowers on his bow ties, not in the paper. He was energetic and bold, constantly searching for ways to shake up the newsroom and the city. He was in charge when the *Globe* hired three baseball-loving sportswriters—Larry Whiteside, Peter Gammons, and Bob Ryan—who would all become Hall of Famers (Ryan, who briefly had the Red Sox as his primary beat, is in the Pro Basketball Hall of Fame). In some cases, they would become as popular and as recognized as the players they covered.

As for the innovation, well, Zim was just getting the surface-level stuff as he drove home with that radio gnawing at him. A couple hours down the road in Connecticut, a 24-hour entertainment and sports TV network was being conceived. ESPN would eventually grow up to be the country's all-day meeting house for sports news and debate. In time, cities of all sizes would have all-sports radio, and the 3-minute TV sports report would appear slow and dated. The news and criticism were going to be traveling at warp speed, and managers were going to have to plan for that as well as the games. They might be able to control a single writer or broadcaster, but they wouldn't be able to manage a team *and* a nonstop news cycle. For longevity, managers would have to change with the times. And although it was the furthest thing from 4-year-old Theo Epstein's mind when he entered Fenway to watch Zim's 1978 team, he would one day understand that managing in Boston goes beyond managing the game.

Three years after young Epstein's first Fenway visit, the past and future of Red Sox management crossed paths in the sprawl of Houston. It was 1981, a year when all of America said "strike" in unison: there was the baseball strike that halved the season, and there was the air traffic controllers' strike, during which 13,000 workers chose to protest rather than punch a clock. The Montreal Expos were playing the Houston Astros on August 19, two and a half weeks after the air strike had started and nine days after the end of the baseball strike.

The Expos' manager was Dick Williams.

Williams had had a few novel experiences while managing the Angels in Disneyland: three consecutive losing seasons, the first three of his managerial career. It wasn't intentional, but he returned to Canada where his success had begun as a manager/light heavyweight in Toronto. He took over the Expos, had two more losing seasons, and then whipped them into one of the best teams in the National League. His team had the speed of Tim Raines, the power of Andre Dawson, the enthusiasm of Gary Carter, and the tolerance of most men in their late 20s who are frequently yelled at by their boss: not much. They were tired of their prickly manager, they complained about him to the front office, and they alternated between playing and waiting for the regime to fall.

On the 19th, the air strike made it difficult to travel from Denver to Houston. There were still flights to be taken, just fewer of them. The Expos' first-round pick from 1980, Terry Francona, had been hitting between .350 and .380 all year in Triple-A Denver and the big club decided it wanted to see him. What timing.

He had been drinking the night before, he was hung over, and—weird as it sounds—it wasn't a good time to be going to the big leagues. He actually told the team trainer that.

"What? You have to go. You're leading off tonight in Houston."

He made arrangements, hopped a series of connections, and finally, in the fifth inning, a cab rolled up to the Astrodome and the slender Francona emerged from the backseat.

Francona was a left-handed hitter with quick wrists, a doubles and gaps man, capable of playing either corner outfield spot. He was the Golden Boy, a hit-maker who never had to be told to keep his hands or his weight back, because he did both naturally. Oh, was it beautiful to watch. He was going to be a star. He was dropped into Double-A Memphis shortly after playing on the Arizona team that won the College World Series, got off to a .160 start in the minors, and still finished the season with a .300 average. The next year he was back in Memphis and, after a hot start, to Denver to play for Felipe Alou. He made the manager's job easy: Francona would lead off against righties and bat eighth or ninth against lefties. He wasn't as fast as Raines, but he ran the bases intelligently and had a dozen triples in Triple-A.

As soon as he made his way to the Expos dugout, he saw his unofficial big brother, Brad Mills. Millsie, his college teammate and roommate, had been drafted by the Expos a year before Francona. He was a rookie, too, having made his big-league debut two months earlier. Millsie and Tim Wallach were screaming his name, and not because they were happy to see him. The manager was trying to get his attention.

"Francona," Williams bellowed. "You're up. You're leading off the next inning."

There was a rush of something, a mixture of nausea and panic, when he heard the instructions. Part of it had to do with him making his debut, and the other part—the nausea part—had a lot to do with the man on the mound, the great Nolan Ryan. Recent strike or not, Ryan could floss his teeth with prospects like Francona. He could break your bat and confidence, and do it with a fastball that traveled at 96 miles per hour on slow days. Francona grabbed a bat and got a break; Ryan was apparently on a pitch count, so Dave Smith faced him instead. He grounded out to second, and the moment seemed to be over in a flash.

The same could be said, really, of his time with Williams. It's not like Francona could talk to him. While he hadn't been around long enough to hate Williams, as some of his teammates did, he saw enough to be intimidated by him. The intimidation wasn't entirely connected to his aura, either. No, what contributed to the stature of Williams was his brain. He had a brilliant baseball mind and knew exactly what he wanted to do two or three innings before it happened. His brain was chocked with notes, pitching matchups he wanted to see, and pinch hitters he wanted to use.

But the information remained locked in that brain. Two and a half weeks after Francona's debut, Williams was fired. If they had talked more, they would have found that they both possessed an overflow passion for baseball. It was a passion so deep that one day it would inspire one of them to go to spring training just weeks after lying in what once appeared to be a deathbed. They both had the type of love for baseball that couldn't be outgrown, and they had hearts that would always make room for the game. There was just one fundamental difference: one man's personality represented the future of baseball managing, and one man's represented the past.

"The drill-sergeant manager doesn't work in this sport anymore," says Jayson Stark, an ESPN baseball writer and commentator. "I ask people all the time to name the last tough guy to win the

World Series. They can't do it. Tony La Russa? Lou Piniella? Nah, they have their soft sides, too. Maybe [former Twins manager] Tom Kelly, but he inspired incredible loyalty from many of those players. So it's a long, long time ago now. A Bill Belichick or a Tom Coughlin—heck, even a Larry Bowa—doesn't fit in this sport anymore."

Epstein wasn't alive when Williams brought his cold-shower style of managing to Boston. And when the 34-year-old Red Sox general manager was an intern in Baltimore, Weaver had been retired for six years. He is asked if either man's style could work in today's Boston.

"In a vacuum? Yes. In the end, we're still talking about ballplayers," he says.

So there's no need for spa language in the clubhouse, no need for egos to be "massaged" and players to be "comfortable"?

"Not in a vacuum," he says, putting an emphasis on the last word.

The last word explains everything.

"Yeah, I absolutely think that in a vacuum, the hardass manager who sort of motivates through fear rather than love could still work in today's game. But we don't live in a vacuum. You can't separate the outside perceptions and the media's perception from the clubhouse environment now. The newspapers are in the clubhouse. The media members linger in the clubhouse. It's not like some outside factor the way it used to be or could be. It's interrelated."

In Boston, sometimes "the media" feels like the entire city. Zim would hate it. His old nemesis Ordway is still on the radio, but with a clearer signal, a larger audience, more co-hosts, and a popular call-in line for the fans—the Whiner Line—created to roast and skewer Boston sports personalities. If only it were as simple as putting the talkers in a sports box: Boston is one of the rare top 15 markets where a sports station, WEEI, is consistently top rated among 25- to 54-year-old men and *all* adults. These are the people who plan summer vacations and summer weddings around the Red Sox's schedule. A smart organization understands that it can manipulate that popularity to serve its interests. Sometimes. In rough moments, when a free agent hasn't played up to expectations or the team has lost five consecutive games, there is no way to tell the people to talk about something else. There are more newspaper writers, from more cities in New England, willing to write about more things related to the team. There are daily and weekly wrap-up shows that comment on all things Red Sox. The players, manager, and general manager are stars; those who cover them are public figures who are quasi-celebrities, gaining their fame from simply covering those on the A-list. There are even Web sites designed to watch those who watch the Red Sox.

"Do you know what the Red Sox have done?" says Gabe Kapler, the former Boston outfielder. "They've created one of the most powerful brands in sports. If you're someone like [*Boston Globe* columnist] Dan Shaughnessy or [*Boston Herald* reporter] Michael Silverman, just having your name associated with the Red Sox gives a major boost to your profile."

Today, Remy is not identified as the second baseman who was pulled aside by Williams. He is not the second baseman who was an All-Star for Zim in 1978. Rather, fans in New England recognize him as the popular analyst from the New England Sports Network. From that perch, he talks insightfully about the game—a must in Boston—and also sprinkles in information about his travels, his favorite TV shows, and the latest products on his Web site. His voice is as powerful as anyone's in the media, so if he is critical of a manager—as he was of former Boston managers Kevin Kennedy and Joe Kerrigan—his commentary tends to hover longer than the average newspaper column or radio tirade. In Boston and in all major cities where people care about baseball, the modern manager at least has to have a daily plan for dealing with the media, even if part of the plan is to simply ignore some of the opinion-makers.

When the Franconas got to Philadelphia, Jacque and Terry were told not to listen to WIP, the all-sports radio station. Francona didn't stick to the advice, although his poker and golf buddy from the Phillies, Bill Giles, wished he had.

"I haven't listened to WIP in 20 years," Giles, the team's chairman, says now. "I hate that station. If somebody tries to call in to say something nice, they won't let them on the air. I really believe that the station does damage to the sports teams here."

If that's ever the case, in Philadelphia, Boston, New York, or Chicago, it's the responsibility of today's manager to at least have an awareness of it or perhaps some type of defense against it. Francona meets with members of the media daily, at 3:30, and isn't above telling them when he disagrees with a position that they've taken. A few times a year, he'll read an article in which a reporter takes the manager to task for a stupid managerial move. If it's a reporter that the manager likes, he might pull him aside and say, "Why didn't you ask me about it after the game? I think I could have given you an explanation that might have changed your opinion."

The job descriptions have changed for everyone around the ballpark. The media are tougher. The GMs are more visible and more accountable. And the relationship between the men inside the clubhouses, players and managers, are more complex than ever. Mark Shapiro, the Cleveland GM, includes "managing personalities" when he is asked to describe the duties of a manager. A grasp of baseball nuance and public relations is expected, as is a willingness to be open to statistical information. Although the Red Sox have Bill James working for them, it's not as if they are the only team with a library of numerical data: It's hard for a manager to justify not considering numbers when fans can easily go to sites such as ESPN.com and baseball-reference.com to get almost any breakdown they can dream up.

Then, after viewing the numbers, a manager has to make sure his interpretation is open-minded, too.

"You still have guys in this sport who manage on instinct," says Stark. "But the best managers in this era study info and use it. For example, if your managing philosophy is still to automatically bring in a left-handed reliever to face a left-handed hitter, even if it's a left-hander who lets left-handed hitters bat .340 against him, you're probably in the wrong profession."

There are exceptions, of course. Bobby Cox is believed to be the best manager in the business, and he broke into the managing game in the same year Zim was talking back to Ordway on the radio. In 1978, the 37-year-old Cox took over the Braves. He stayed there for five seasons, left for the Blue Jays and Toronto, and then returned to Atlanta in 1990. Cox can say that he managed first-place teams in his 40s, 50s, and 60s. He was in charge when the Braves, in 14 consecutive non-strike seasons, finished atop their division. It's hard to categorize Cox as belonging to any particular school. At some point in his career, he has probably been both trend and dinosaur. He'll be back in Atlanta in 2008—he turns 67 in May—for his 28th season of managing.

"There's much more raw material out there for people to evaluate the manager and second-guess," Epstein says. "I don't think the perspective of the critics has improved. I just think there's more fuel for the fire. There is no more insight, per se. Being second-guessed as the manager by the public is never fun and it makes it more frequent or intense than it ever was before. . . . It makes interacting with the media and the public more challenging."

In Boston, the job is not for a man, or a family, with thin skin. When Francona's daughter, Leah, started Brookline High School in September 2004, she was blindsided in an English class: The teacher wanted the students to write a persuasive paper, and just in case the class didn't understand what he meant by "persuasive," he offered an example: "You could write an essay detailing why Terry Francona should be fired as manager of the Red Sox." The girl went pale. Did this mean she had no chance of passing this class? After Leah got to know her school and her city better, she understood that the Red Sox were just part of the conversation; the teacher, who meant no malice, turned out to be one of her favorites.

Managing in Boston would be miserable for a man who needs just 10 minutes of silence so he can make decisions in peace. It is not the position for one who believes his word should be accepted as final, with no debate. There is no final word, and there's always, always a debate. Following the Red Sox is, as Epstein puts it, "a running dialogue." It's so much of a dialogue that Epstein sometimes changes the subject when friends and family members bring up the team when he is allegedly off the clock. If he happens to be on an airplane and the person next to him asks what he does, he says, "I'm in the concrete business." Concrete is a conversation-stopper; sitting next to the GM of the Red Sox, though, leads to an open-ended conversation.

On most days, being popular is a good thing for those who work for the Red Sox. The resources are plentiful, and the payroll ensures that the team will always have a chance to win. Popularity also guarantees instant analysis and instant ridicule for the manager; his explanations can wait until the morning.

To do the job well, you have to love baseball more than you love anything else. To be a city's well-paid punching bag, sometimes you have to love baseball more than you love yourself.

CHAPTER 4

Falling Stars

This was his life plan, not his dream, and he didn't have to explain the distinction to many people in New Brighton, Pennsylvania. It didn't matter that the man with the plan was actually a 9-year-old boy. There were none of those condescending pats on the head when the plan was mentioned around adults.

Terry Francona was going to be a big-league ballplayer.

A dream? No, you can outgrow some dreams and be snapped out of and awakened from others. This plan was as solid as the grand pianos that his grandfather, Carmen, tuned in town. It was as clear as Carmen's booming voice—no mike necessary—when he preached to his congregation, the Italian Christian Center, at the corner of 5th Street and 8th Avenue.

Grandpa was on board, and not just because his son, Tito, already was in the big leagues. Anyone could see that the kid was devoted to the game. He worked at it, craved it, and could only be pulled away from it when he heard Tito's piercing, two-finger whistle, which meant it was time to run home immediately. He could be in the middle of a great game with the neighborhood kids, and he'd drop everything and sprint once he heard that whistle. Tito and Birdie's only son had it figured out early: he didn't spend his energy disobeying his folks; there was too much work to do.

That work began at home one summer, when Tito was away playing for the Atlanta Braves of Hank Aaron, Joe Torre, and Felipe Alou. Terry came across a contest sponsored by Phillips 66. He perked up when he read that the contest was for kids his age, and the purpose was to find out who had the best pitching, catching, and hitting skills. Birdie, God bless her, couldn't play catch with him to help hone his skills for the contest. But she was resourceful enough to take an old trash can, a net, and some concrete and build her son a homemade contraption that would help him practice his throwing and catching.

She finished building the mechanical practice partner, and her son became the only 9-year-old in western Pennsylvania with a full-time job. He threw at it daily, determined to be better than everyone else. When the big day arrived, Birdie drove him to town and the two of them watched and talked as dozens of fathers and sons got in their last-minute practice throws. Mother and son spent their time telling stories, and when it was time to perform, Terry put on a show. He blew away the field, and now it was time to take home the first-place . . .

Uh-oh. What was this? He saw the organizers of the event huddling, pointing, and shaking their heads. What was going on? Turns out, they told Birdie, that they were going to have to disqualify her son because of who his father was. Since he was the son of a big-league player, he was deemed to have an unfair advantage over the other participants.

Birdie was furious. What did that have to do with how hard her son had worked? His father was with the Braves all summer, and she hadn't coached him up, either. She was a saint—her son joked that he wasn't sure how she ever got pregnant—but even saints have fuses. First she promised to write letters to all of the higher-ups at Phillips 66. Then she got so angry that hot tears welled in her eyes. She and her son got back in the car to head home. He had simply wanted to prove that he could smoke the other kids—he couldn't have cared less about that first-place trophy. Birdie asked him if an ice cream cone would make things better (he said yes), and she continued to vent about the gall of those organizers. She drove with two hands clenched on the wheel, eyes locked on the road, mumbling about the injustice they had just experienced. And then Terry spoke up.

"Mom?" he said.

"Yes?"

"Why are we in Ohio?"

Indeed, she had been so agitated that she had driven into the neighboring state. They both laughed. He had traveled for baseball before, but not quite like that. His traveling had been to the city where his father was playing ball.

Tito Francona was a lefty outfielder and first baseman who had produced his best season in 1959, the year his son was born. He was a 90-minute drive from home, in Cleveland, and he hit as if Municipal Stadium were one of the local Beaver County parks. In 1959, the general rule was that if he was swinging, he was also connecting, and the ball was most likely landing somewhere safely: he hit .415 at home, .363 overall, and finished fifth in MVP voting. By the time Terry was old enough to hang out with him at the ballpark, in the mid-1960s, his father was moving toward the end of his career.

Not that it bothered Terry. Each June, the Franconas would spend 3 months in the city where Tito was playing. Whether that was St. Louis, Atlanta, Oakland, or Milwaukee, it was 3 months of being around Dad and baseball. Terry would wake up early, go outside, and look for a game to play. If no one was around, he'd take his ball and glove and play catch with the concrete walls of whatever apartment complex they were renting.

When it was time to go the park, he'd hop in the backseat and listen to his father and some carpooling teammates talk shop. They'd arrive at the stadium at 2:30, and Tito would give his son a daily refreshment budget of one dollar. The players got used to seeing him around, even if all of them didn't know his name. They used shorthand—Little Tito—and the nickname stuck. Terry would shag flies when he was allowed, and sit in the stands when he wasn't. As game time approached, he'd often choose the 75-cent chicken fillet, add a Coke, and study the game. He sat in the wives' section, and he found that they talked too much for his enjoyment. He'd sit there, quietly absorbing more game details than his father realized.

One August night in 1970, Tito's final season, the Brewers were playing the stacked Minnesota Twins. It would have been easy for an 11-year-old boy's mind to drift: Tito's Brewers were on their way to 97 losses and the Twins were charging toward 98 wins. They had stars like Tony Oliva, Harmon Killebrew, and the lefty with the delightful swing, Rod Carew. But Terry wasn't as intrigued by them as he was by the man on the mound. It was a 19-year-old Bert Blyleven, whose impact went beyond his 12 strikeouts and complete-game victory.

"Dad," an amazed Terry said as they were on their way home, "that was one of the best breaking balls I've ever seen."

Tito paused. His son really had been paying attention, because young Blyleven was on his way to fashioning one of the best curveballs in baseball. It was also obvious how much his son wanted to be a part of the game. He had never, ever pushed baseball on him, yet that's all Terry thought about, even after Tito retired.

Their son's singular focus was one of the reasons Tito and Birdie had peace in their ranch-style home. They were spared a lot of adolescence's rebellion and drama because Terry wasn't going to be derailed from his baseball plan. In fact, he didn't even *know* that he could be derailed. He didn't particularly enjoy going to class, but he did well in school because he knew that poor grades would take away baseball.

He managed to simultaneously amuse and frustrate his high school guidance counselor, Rico Antonini. Each year, starting in ninth grade, students were required to fill out a sheet with their career intentions listed on it. Each year, Terry Francona gave the same answer: *I'm going to be a professional baseball player.* Mr. Antonini's response was exasperation the first couple of years, and then understanding after he saw what everyone else in town did. Tito's son—Terry, "T," Little Tito—was good.

Anyway, Mr. Antonini should have noticed that Terry was surrounding himself with a group of high achievers, kids who were well on their way to being established in diverse fields. Some of the kids he played pickup ball with, kids like Bruce Schwartzel and Brian Lambert, Tad Mackowicki and Mike Pasquale, had a drive to be great, too. Schwartzel, his next-door neighbor on Mercer Road, probably had an idea back in the 1970s that he would grow up to take over the family's plumbing business. Lambert, who lived two doors down, was on the path to becoming an eye doctor in New Brighton. Mackowicki displayed the savvy that would one day allow him to have a television production company. And it was clear that Pasquale would become a surgeon, especially after the time they all got in trouble and Pasquale cried out, "I'm not going to get into medical school now!"

If they could work toward their careers, Terry could do the same with his. He was too polite to boast, but they all recognized his disarming smirk. It was their reminder that he never thought he was going to lose. His thoughts were usually correct.

"He came to me as a perfect hitter," says Greg Fazio, his high school baseball coach. "So when he was a sophomore, I told him he'd have to learn to pitch, too." He did learn to pitch: his earned run average was 0.33, he threw a no-hitter, and he hit .550.

No one denied that talent and good genes were part of his story. Pro baseball has more father-son combinations than any other sport. But he was exceptional in the categories in which gene pools offer no guarantees. He had Tito's gift *and* Carmen's self-made grit. When his grandfather wasn't taking a hammer to the pianos until they sounded just right, he was off in the hills, covered in the grime of the local steel mills. And when he wasn't there, he was preaching church services in Italian and English, too. He was always on some clock, even when a time card said he wasn't.

His grandson saw the effort and respected it. In a sense he copied it, because a running clock and the nonstop sweat that accompanied it didn't bother him. Fazio learned that it was simple for Terry to accept that baseball practice had a beginning and middle, but he totally rejected the concept of an end. Those closest to him knew that there was a lot of heat lurking beneath his easy smile and jokes. He often thought that he could will himself to be successful, probably because he never met failure in any sport.

He liked basketball enough, but didn't have a deep passion for it, yet he still could score 20 points in a flash as a 6-foot guard on the New Brighton team. He went out for the golf team as a freshman, made it, and became the school's best golfer. He was 3 years younger than Joe Montana and 2 years older than Dan Marino— both western Pennsylvania quarterbacks—and he thought of playing football like them, but his father talked him out of it.

Really, his best work was done underground. Between his sophomore and junior seasons, he turned the family basement into a baseball compound. This kid, with his long hair parted down the middle and red Chuck Taylor sneakers on his feet, had a work ethic that defied his hang-loose exterior. He'd set up his stereo, give some volume to Aerosmith, and practice his swing with a lead bat. There was a light hanging in the basement, and he practiced his throws by perfecting his arm slot so that he could hit the strike zone, formed on cement blocks, and avoid the light. Day after day, Birdie and Tito heard *Toys in the Attic* and baseball in the basement.

All that work led to a season in which getting Terry out was worthy of a headline. Pitchers got him out just nine times in 1976, when he hit .769.

As hard as he worked and as respectful as he was, he was still a teenager. He and his buddies were hanging out at the New Brighton Hot Dog Shop one day, eating away. Then they figured out that they didn't have any money. So they slipped out without paying and headed to Pappan's, a family-owned diner in town. The three of them sat in a booth and began looking at a menu, and soon a nice man joined them. He was a police officer. He casually picked up a menu, looked at it, and said to the group, "I think you boys must have forgotten to pay at the Hot Dog Shop; can you take care of that for me?" They rounded up some cash and paid their bill.

It was hard to get away with much in New Brighton. The town was so small and friendly that Terry didn't have to drive anywhere if he didn't want to; he could go to the end of his driveway, hold up his thumb, and someone passing by would take him where he needed to go. It was small enough that when Terry was supposed to be eating lunch at school and instead traveled to a place called Eat 'N Park, he ran into the mayor at the time, Paul Spickerman, and the mayor recognized him.

There were moments when he had Tito pacing in the living room, just waiting for him to return home after being out with his friends. That's exactly what happened one night when Tito's antennae went up early: he became suspicious when he saw his son's car parked in the church parking lot. Terry had left the car door open, with the keys inside, with a note to his girlfriend. He wanted her to drive his car and meet him at a party. Tito got the note and keys before his son's girlfriend did. The good news was that at least Terry's car hadn't careened into the ditch that his friend's had. The news that would eventually get Terry grounded for a month was that he was in a car with a few other guys, and they had all been drinking.

There weren't many positive things about that night, but there were a couple. One was that no one got hurt in the accident. The other was . . . well, Mr. Wooley's wife. Mr. Wooley, a young English teacher, had always told his students that if they were ever in any kind of trouble, they should contact him promptly. Since they were in trouble—a car in a ditch is real trouble—they went to his house, banging on the door at midnight. They had always talked about how good looking the teacher's wife was, and to their surprise, guess who was answering the door in a negligee?

"Whatever happens to me tonight, it's almost worth it after seeing this," Terry said.

It was a line, but he knew it wasn't true. He was going to have problems at home. As he drove back to his house with teammate Johnny Albanese, he kept repeating that his father was going to kill him. Albanese told him not to worry because they always had the option of running away from home. Terry didn't listen. "My dad is going to kick my ass," he said. Albanese offered a few more options as he pulled into the Franconas' driveway. And when he saw an angry man waiting by that front door, he barely waited for Terry to close the passenger door before he peeled out of that driveway and into the night. So much for the runaway plan; Terry would have to handle it alone.

Tito waited for his son to slog up the driveway. As soon as the door opened, Tito picked Terry up—he had meant to drag him—and took him to the kitchen for a real talking-to. Mom and Dad mentioned taking baseball away from him, but Terry got off with the far easier sentence: a month of no social activities.

Besides, the professional scouts and college coaches would have been disappointed if that had been the end of his baseball career. He was going to be drafted, and he was going to be pursued by some of the top college programs in the country. He heard from Florida State, North Carolina, Wichita State, and Arizona. Of all of them, boy, did he ever love North Carolina. On a visit there, he was able to see a basketball game at the famous Carmichael Auditorium. It was beautiful to be sitting near a court, trimmed in baby blue, watching players like Phil Ford and Mike O'Koren carry out Dean Smith's instructions. The head baseball coach, Mike Roberts, was a young guy and Terry would be one of his first recruits.

That was the plan in his heart, and although clichés celebrate romantic decisions, Terry's unemotional baseball sensibilities knew what was best. If he wanted to stay on the sure big-league path, it probably made more sense to sign with either the University of Arizona or with the Chicago Cubs, who had taken him in the second round of the 1977 draft. Arizona's head coach was Jerry Kindall, who had played in Cleveland with Tito. Despite that, Coach Kindall was blunt in a phone conversation with Fazio: "We don't recruit in Pennsylvania." What he should have added was that the Wildcats didn't normally recruit there. They were going beyond making an exception for Terry; he had never seen the school and they had never seen him play. In both cases, with individual and institution, their reputations had preceded them.

As summer got closer to fall, the Cubs were making Terry's decision even easier. The magic number in his head was $40,000.

If the Cubs weren't willing to give him that to sign, he would pack up and fly to Tucson. The Cubs offered $18,000 and then upped their offer—$19,000!—before school started. *Oh, well,* he thought. *What a wasted draft pick.* He was going to Arizona.

He was alone when he flew to Tucson as a prized 18-year-old recruit. He had made the decision to attend Arizona and reject the insulting Cubs offer, and those were both grown-up decisions. But he was a kid, in body and in thought. Wait until the people in Arizona saw that they were pinning part of their future on a 6-foot-1, 160-pound package of bones. He wasn't ready for the college fastball, he wasn't prepared for the college workload, and he wasn't prepared to be away from home. Back in New Brighton he had a cute girl-friend, a stable home life, and an entire town that supported him.

What had he done? He spent a lot of time on one of those dormitory pay phones, leaning against the wall and crying to his folks. The other top recruit, a junior college transfer named Brad Mills, was nothing like him. This guy was serious: he was 2 years older, he was stronger, he was organized, and he was already en-gaged to be married. Mills had looked forward to meeting the Terry Francona that everyone had raved about, and when he fi-nally saw him, frankly, he thought the program was in trouble. In his opinion, those red Chuck Taylors were a pair of red flags.

Neither recruit had any idea how much their baseball lives were going to change under Kindall. He was a stickler for fundamentals, and he'd hold practices for 4½ hours sometimes. He knew every-thing there was to know about baseball, and his mission was to make sure his players did, too. If they missed anything, they'd re-peat a drill.

Terry got better fast under Kindall, so much so that he was a starter in left field as a freshman. Still, it seemed that everything in college was faster, and that wasn't always positive. Just as he was

feeling good about his freshman year and his now-close relationship
to teammate and roommate Mills, here was Coach Kindall with
something else at the end of the year: his young left fielder had been
invited to participate in summer baseball in Fairbanks, Alaska. It
was a great opportunity.

"Coach, I know it sounds good," Terry said. "But I haven't
seen my family."

The coach was direct: "Do you want to be a real player or not?"

He went back to New Brighton for 5 days, said hello to his
parents and good-bye to his girlfriend, and went to play in Alaska.
From Alaska he went to play with the USA Team in Italy. From
Italy he went back to Arizona. Not much changed after his sophomore year, when his featured international baseball trip was Cuba,
where he looked into Fidel Castro's eyes and shook his hand. He
was getting his first taste of big-league life: there is no such thing
as summer vacation.

While he was in Cuba, one of his friends—they called him the
Riddler—was working on his behalf in Tucson. As a freshman,
Terry had been in a methods of mathematics class with a couple of
attractive girls from Tucson. He once had the nerve to pass them,
hand them a note on his way by, and keep walking. They looked at
the note, looked at each other, and then cracked up laughing. Of
course, the joke started with the shoes and moved up to the hair,
which they believed was 2 or 3 years behind the times.

Anyway, that had been 2 years earlier. The Riddler saw one of
the girls, Jacque Lang, and told her that one of his friends thought
she was great. The problem, the Riddler explained, was that he
was too afraid to ask her out. Terry got back to Tucson, heard the
story, and called Jacque Lang to apologize for his clumsy friend.
And then he asked her out.

She was cute and smart, an Arizona cheerleader with her mind on medical school. Their first date was at the Lunt Avenue Marble Club, and the date was sponsored by Grandpa Francona. Every time Terry hit a home run, Carmen would send him $10. Sometimes it seemed that Terry would round third and dial home: "Gramps, I hit a home run today . . . Can you get it here tomorrow?" Ten bucks could get you a whole lot of appetizers, including the fried zucchini and ranch dip that they ate that night.

What a date. They both should have had "Rx" printed on their shirts. Jacque was wearing a cast because she had fallen from a cheerleading pyramid. Terry was going to have his wisdom teeth removed and was given ominous instructions: "Try not to breathe on anybody." He liked her a lot, and he allowed his thoughts to consider marriage when she wasn't thinking that way at all. He may have even been thinking of marriage on that first date when, driving in his 1975 Mustang, he was talking to her so much that he rear-ended the car in front of him. At least he made her laugh. No damage, no injuries, and a relationship was born.

Terry was a dominating presence on Coach Kindall's team by this time. He had played a lot of baseball over the summers, and he had grown into his lanky body. He hadn't lifted many weights, and he still had packed 25 pounds onto his physique. While his freshman year was marked by a high batting average but little impact on the game, he was a middle-of-the-order contributor as a junior. There were just two issues with the season.

One was that it was the first he played without Mills, who had become an unlikely member of his family. They couldn't have been more different on the surface. They had been roommates for road games, presumably so Coach Kindall could teach the players to get along with their alter egos. Mills was the neat freak, the one who could take one look at his pens and folders and instantly know if they had been moved 2 inches to the left or right. He had those supplies because, long before laptops, he was keeping impeccably handwritten files on opponents and their tendencies. He was as precise, organized, and talented as any hitter who had ever come through Tucson. The first few games Terry watched him play, he said to himself, "This is the best hitter I've ever seen."

Mills began his Arizona career by hitting well over .400, but a shoulder injury slowed his production and concerned the scouts. They still liked the ability, and they would have had their evaluation cards revoked if they hadn't, but the injury added more risk to the already risky world of amateur drafting.

The other "issue" Terry had was taken care of in a 5-minute conversation with Kindall. The coach was worried that his star player might be too infatuated with Jacque, and that the infatuation would take his mind off baseball. Coaches can sense the difference between a fling and a future, and what Terry had for Ms. Lang was no fling.

"It's still me, Coach," Terry reminded him. "I can't believe you're having this conversation with me: I'm always here two hours early."

The kid was right. His passion for baseball was overflowing; it was probably a good thing if he used some of that overflow passion to fall in love. It certainly wasn't affecting his game or the team's fortunes. They were favorites in the College World Series and Terry was the College Player of the Year. Mills was already in the pros, drafted in the 17th round by the Expos, and Terry was going to be joining him soon.

It seemed too staged that the Expos would draft him, too, but with the 22nd pick of the first round, one spot ahead of a high school prospect named Billy Beane. The draft happened, Arizona won the title, and Coach Kindall pulled him aside.

"I think you know what you have to do now," the coach said. "It's probably time for you to move on and take this opportunity."

Terry Francona was closer to being a big-league ballplayer.

He flew home from Omaha, site of the World Series, with his parents. Jacque still had to finish school at Arizona, but he knew that the start of his pro career was not going to mean an ending for them. It couldn't; she had no idea how close he was to asking her to marry him. But before that could happen, he had to sign a deal. He was a young man now, a man whose vision was even sharper than that of the 18-year-old kid who had been bold enough to turn down the $19,000 from the Cubs. It was 1980, his draft status had changed, and the price of doing business had gone up. His price: $100,000 on the nose.

The deal was completed over one of Birdie's turkey dinners, and a few hours later Terry was on his way to Pittsburgh International Airport for a flight to Memphis, where he would begin his Double-A career. Tito gave him the advice of a veteran baseball man: "Son, see the ball and hit the ball." Birdie gave him tears and a head shake: "You are now a piece of meat." She was grateful that he had been given his father's gift, but gifts sometimes have hidden pouches of pain. He was in a fragile place now, and she knew it. It was a place where his first love now doubled as his business, and like love, business is often irrational. She had helped raise an innocent boy with an innocent love for a sport. Now love was going to be on a contract.

There's something about mothers: part protectors, part prophets. As Terry drove in Ugly Duckling rental cars, stayed in Admiral Benbow Hotels, and stretched out on pool rafts atop the floors of Greyhound buses—he had to get comfortable somehow—he often wondered what he had gotten himself into. How many reminders did he need that this was not the baseball bubble of Coach Kindall's Arizona?

Maybe it was the time he saw his manager, Larry Bearnarth,

charge from the first seat of the bus toward the last, with designs on fighting a player. (They were separated, so the manager with the degree in English literature didn't have a fight story for his memoirs.) Maybe it was the time he drove in a run and was told by one of the veterans, "You had better thank him." Thank him? For what? Aren't you supposed to come home from second on a single? It could have been the bus rides for trips that would have been flights in college: ten hours from Memphis to Savannah, twelve hours—Lord, have mercy—from Memphis to Orlando.

Honestly, it could have been his game. All anyone told him was to hit .300, and if he did that he'd be fine. He did it, but he didn't like the way it was done. He was a velvet hammer tapping away in the middle of Graceland. He didn't want to keep stacking harmless singles after harmless singles.

Things got better in his second season, when he returned to Memphis and then was summoned to Triple-A Denver. He was told to keep his apartment in Memphis because he wouldn't be in Colorado long. The words were right and wrong: He got four hits in his first Triple-A game, and Alou, his father's former teammate, wasn't going to let him go back to Double-A. The manager could see that Little Tito knew what he was doing at the plate; he was so good that Alou let him put on the hit-and-run by himself. He'd tug on his helmet, and that was the sign for the runner. He was so good that he could watch the middle infielders break and hit the ball where they weren't. If the shortstop slid over to cover, he'd slap the ball past him, too.

Alou was a fun and unusual manager to play for. While some managers needed to have their obvious fingerprints on the game, Alou's ego didn't get in the way of what was best for the team. If he trusted the player, he understood that the player could see certain things that the manager couldn't.

So they all had a blast in the thin air of Denver, with each day bringing a satchel full of hits. When the Expos called for Terry in the summer of '81, it was the last time he'd see his apartments in Memphis and Denver. Heading toward 1982, his life was all about making things official: He was officially a big-league player and, three months shy of his 23rd birthday, he and Jacque could officially refer to themselves as Mr. and Mrs. Terry Francona.

They were married in Tucson and Grandpa Francona performed the ceremony. The family had seen Carmen do weddings before, and they gently reminded Terry that there had been some flubbed names and comical lapses during big moments. Terry didn't care. He insisted on having his grandfather bring them together. A mispronounced name or procedure out of order wasn't going to stop the marriage. The point was having Grandpa there, and as his grandson expected, the ceremony was flawless.

If only events on the field could be described the same way, for Terry and Mills.

For Millsie, the worst parts of his collegiate career trailed him to the big leagues. If it wasn't a shoulder it was a knee, and if it wasn't a knee it was a random line drive hitting him in Houston. It was always something masking all that talent, and then, cruelly, it was always something taking away from it. The same player who had been good enough to jump from Double-A to the big leagues and hit .300 had been transformed into a comeback player. He was always coming back from some injury, trying to regain his stroke in the majors until the injuries forced him, permanently, to the minors.

For Terry, 1982 changed his life. At 22, it's natural to think of an arc on the rise. No one peaks at 22, so there is a gaze toward tomorrow and an excitement about what it might bring. Who would imagine that the very first month of the year would contain the most joy? Terry married that beautiful girl and he made it to the big leagues, so now the plan was framed nicely, just as he always knew it would be. But that was just the snapshot, and all the sadness was in the moving pictures.

The year was intent on reshaping Terry, and this time fate met him somewhere he always was: at the ballpark. It was June 16, in left field, and the Cardinals were involved in the lesson. The Expos were at a wet Busch Stadium, and thanks to eight runs in the first three innings, they were coasting in St. Louis. Terry, with a .321 average, was an everyday player for Montreal. Even with the soggy track in a runaway game, he was also an every-inning player for the Expos.

The warning track at Busch was still holding water from a previous storm, and that was the problem as Terry went back to retrieve a rare double by light-hitting utility man Julio Gonzalez. That ball was smoked, and as Terry turned for it, part of the track came up. He lost his balance and crashed into the wall. He felt his knee explode then, and the pain was excruciating. It was odd: as he went back to the dugout, he was suddenly embarrassed that he had made such a production on the field. The knee didn't hurt as much as it had minutes earlier, although he couldn't turn on it.

It was a torn anterior cruciate ligament. His season was over. The good news was that the injury was not career-ending, at least not in the way that most people understand the term. It didn't end his career as a player, but it was the first step to ending it as a starter. It was also the beginning of a lifelong struggle with his legs. He began his rehab as soon as he was cleared, and that didn't surprise anyone. He'd do anything to get back on the field, to get back to competing.

In September, though, Terry put his rehab on pause. Carmen Francona, in his dress shirt, slacks, and black shoes, went to the basement as he always did and turned on an old radio. The Cardinals and

Expos were playing, and even without an injured Terry on the field, Grandpa wanted to listen. Oh, was he proud. His grandson was making a living at the game he loved, and getting a lot of crisp ten-dollar bills to do it. That game marked the last time Carmen Francona, father and grandfather to a pair of big-leaguers, could check up on his grandson's team. He had a heart attack later that night, and the heart attack took his life.

Carmen's passing wasn't just about the passing of a family's patriarch. He was literally the voice of a town, tuning those pianos and then singing along as he got the pitch just right. He was the one who could make you laugh, unintentionally, when he sang in church and his voice drowned out the music, no matter how loud that music was. If you met him just once, he was your buddy. If you saw him again, he was probably your best friend. He was the reason people in western Pennsylvania initially thought of music and preaching, not baseball, when they heard the Francona name.

Later that fall, Terry visited his parents in New Brighton. He was still rehabbing, but he felt much better physically than he had in months. He told Tito and Birdie that he was going out to the road behind their house to run. They peered out the windows and watched him laboring back there, going up and down the road, running like someone who didn't make a living as a professional baseball player. He looked horrible. And that wasn't even the worst part of the story. After a while, he returned to the house and gave his analysis of what he had just done.

"Dad, I felt great out there," he said. "I'm almost there."

Tito couldn't tell him just then how bad he looked, and Birdie could only cry. He was 23, and he looked like an old man running out there. They could see it, but he couldn't. Birdie probably knew right then that he'd have a full baseball life, just not the one that he had expected.

CHAPTER 5

Managing Jordan

The news broke on a Tuesday night, and as it buzzed its way through Chicago, there wasn't a soul in the city who looked forward to facing Wednesday morning. This was the king of all scoops, so it was appropriate that it took the strength of three media outlets—NBC, the *Chicago Sun-Times*, and the *Denver Post*—to simultaneously carry it to the public: Michael Jordan was going to wake up on October 6, 1993, and announce his retirement from pro basketball and the Chicago Bulls.

Jordan was in his prime as an athlete and as a stylist and pitchman, too. His team had won the previous three NBA titles and was favored to secure a fourth. He was the finals MVP in each championship year, and he had averaged at least 30 points per game in the previous three seasons. His elevation of basketball was literal, and he was the only athlete for whom the following statement was true: he couldn't follow the trends of pop culture because those trends were too busy following him, from his bald head to the Air Jordans on his feet. The cliché of commissioners is that their leagues are stronger than one superstar, but Jordan wore the NBA's crown, was its most charmed and recognized face, and was its proof that ferocity could be perfectly blended with grace.

The 250 reporters who covered his retirement press conference were familiar with the highlights of Jordan's résumé, so they essentially remixed one question—why?—and asked it several different ways over the course of an hour. His comment that there was nothing "left to prove" didn't seem believable, especially given his thirst for any type of competition, so they pressed. They asked if his decision had anything to do with the death of his father, James, who had been murdered by two North Carolina teenagers 3 months earlier. They asked about themselves, knowing that Jordan had been annoyed by the media's scrutiny of his gambling appetite in general and, specifically, his gambling trip to Atlantic City the night before a playoff game in New York. They asked, simply, what he planned to do next.

"The word 'retire' means you can do whatever you feel like doing," he said. "I'm going to sit there and watch the grass grow. When it needs mowing, I'll get up and cut it."

Well, not exactly. The season began without Jordan, and while the Bulls of Scottie Pippen and Horace Grant were not a great team, they were good enough to have won two-thirds of their games going into New Year's Day 1994. At the same time, rumors about early retiree Jordan began to circulate. He wasn't content to watch the grass grow, so he was looking for a patch of outfield grass on which to run. Michael Jordan, who was basketball's best player even when he was sitting on his couch, wanted to play baseball.

The news of Jordan's retirement had led sports columnists to write glowing tributes, but there was no love or tolerance for this baseball business. Baseball? Jordan hadn't played the sport with any type of regularity since he was a skinny 16-year-old kid in North

Carolina. How was he supposed to take a 14-year break from the game and still be able to hit a curveball? How was he going to be able to do his favorite thing—compete—when he hadn't played baseball in college and never spent a day in the minor leagues? For Jordan, each day produced a new question, and each article and broadcast offered unsolicited advice. *Don't do it, Mike. And come back to the NBA.*

If Bulls owner Jerry Reinsdorf was having those thoughts, his actions didn't show it. Reinsdorf also owned the White Sox, who were a few weeks away from beginning spring training in Sarasota, Florida. Since ending their 1993 season with a loss in the American League Championship Series, the White Sox had made a number of moves in free agency. They re-signed Tim Raines, and added designated hitter Julio Franco and outfielder Darrin Jackson. They also signed Jordan to a minor league contract.

The plan was for him to rub shoulders with White Sox stars like Frank Thomas, Jack McDowell, and Robin Ventura, and then be assigned to a team in the minors. He had no chance of being the team's fourth outfielder, utility man, or 25th player. Baseball people love to talk about a prospect's "makeup," and Jordan was a plus in that category. But he was a long and busy symphony of arms and legs at the plate, with no form or game plan. He was raw, and he needed work in every area just to keep from embarrassing the organization and himself.

One morning in Sarasota, the White Sox's entire baseball staff met in the trailer that served as their temporary office. It was just after 7:00, and a bleary Terry Francona was asleep with his eyes open. He was the 34-year-old manager of Chicago's Double-A affiliate, the Birmingham Barons. The previous year, in his first season of managing Birmingham, his Barons had won the Southern League championship. *Baseball America* named him its Minor

League Manager of the Year, one year after it had given the same honor to the Greenville Braves' Grady Little. He was highly regarded in the organization, probably more than he knew, because his bosses had just said something that gave him a jolt for the rest of the meeting and season. They were putting Jordan's development in his hands.

"MJ's going to Birmingham," they said to him. "So be heads-up and don't say anything stupid."

"Okay," Francona replied. "I can handle it. No big deal."

When he opened the door of that trailer, he was forced to become a different manager. Had he actually said, "No big deal"? Yeah, right. There were reporters and camera crews already waiting to talk to him, because they had gotten the word before he had. This was going to be nothing like his first year in Birmingham, when he called all the beat writers by their first names—all two of them, Wayne and Reuben.

Now that he was managing Jordan, he was going to have to learn, for at least part of the day, to be as organized as his pal Millsie. If this were basketball and he were Phil Jackson, managing Jordan would still be challenging. Jordan in baseball was something entirely different. Francona knew that he was going to have to be alert at 7:00 A.M., thinking about his plans for the team, his plans for Jordan, and his plans for the paparazzi. He was getting Jordan at a time when both men were growing into unfamiliar jobs and dealing with various personal heartbreaks.

Francona had stopped playing baseball 3 years earlier, finally incapable of icing all the things that hurt. In his final season, he had gotten into a routine of dunking his entire body in a whirlpool in an attempt to soothe the pain. After his first ACL injury in 1982, he was able to come back in 1984 and hit .346 in the first 3 months of the Expos' season. Then, on June 14, almost

2 years to the day of his injury in St. Louis, his other knee exploded against the Pirates. John Tudor was pitching for Pittsburgh that day, and when Tudor went to cover first base, he said he could hear the sickening pop that caused Francona's knee to collapse.

Maybe he could have adjusted to one ACL injury, but not two. He truly needed to have reconstructive knee surgery, but he worked around it. He could no longer think of being a special hitter because he had no sturdy leg base; he couldn't expect to be a full-time player because he couldn't stay on the field.

It was a physical struggle for him to play at all. He wore bulky leg braces and sometimes used four or five rolls of tape to keep his knees in place. He often said to himself, "I'm not a very good player," but he was still the boy in New Brighton who never would have left a baseball game if his father didn't know how to whistle. He still wanted in somehow.

The reality was that he was a bench player in his early 20s, and no matter how great a teammate you are, you don't come to the ballpark at that age expecting to watch the game. There were times on the road when Francona and Expos teammate Chris Speier would be so restless, knowing that they weren't going to play, that they'd drive around searching for competitive pickup basketball games just for a good sweat. A "caged animal" is how Jacque Francona described the player who was losing playing time due to his body's betrayal.

At the end of his career, with his knees and shoulders breaking down, Francona was the happiest ex–big leaguer in Triple-A. He was in Louisville in 1990 and he was getting at bats. (He even pitched seven and two-thirds innings and had an ERA of 1.17.) He became a better evaluator then, too, of himself and other players. He looked at kids like Ray Lankford and Bernard Gilkey and saw that they were better than he was. He also studied manager Gaylen Pitts and noticed how he consistently made tough decisions and still maintained the respect of his players by not embarrassing them.

Francona wanted to be that kind of manager, and now he was getting his chance to learn with Jordan. What better way to fine-tune his skills as a teacher than by imparting the nuances of pro baseball into a pro basketball player? Is there a better way to balance the interests of big-city media versus the interests of the team than to have a graduate course in Dealing with Michael Jordan's Media? Jordan was definitely going to have some rough nights at the park, and yes, even he would be insecure and lose his confidence. No one in Double-A knew how it felt to have Jordan's genius and drive, but Francona knew how everyone felt on a baseball field. He had been all of them: bonus-baby/first-round pick, starter, platoon player, defensive replacement, pinch hitter, player frustrated by injuries, player who sat on the bench without playing for 2 months, player who had been released.

That was just the professional perspective he could give to the world's number-one athlete. He couldn't have conceptualized what their personal relationship would become.

The first time they talked was on that onetime sleepy morning in Sarasota. After Francona learned that he was Jordan's manager, he found him on one of the minor league fields and introduced himself. Jordan was scheduled to play in a game that day, and he was hosting a line of players and coaches who wanted to give him baseball pointers.

"We've got five days until we get to Birmingham, so I'm going to leave you alone for now," Francona said. "There's too much coaching going on here, so go play and we'll talk in depth later."

That was all they said until Francona actually saw Jordan play. He had been jammed on a pitch and popped it up. It was a normal day in the life of a ballplayer, except that Jordan didn't run out the play. As soon as it happened, all heads turned to Francona. Typical: it's easy to be Jordan's coach when you want to teach him how to swing and maybe sneak in a question about the Knicks, but the numbers in the coaching line start and end at "1" when the job requires scolding him.

After the game, they crossed paths on a back field.

"Just tell me now: are you going to do that every time?"

Jordan may have been a baseball rookie, but he knew what Francona was referring to. In basketball, he was able to set the tone for the amount of effort his team exerted because he brought the most passion and, when necessary, fury. He knew he wasn't going to be the best player for the Barons, but he would be their most watched; therefore, he could still determine how hard they worked.

"No, that will never happen again," he said, his dark brown eyes making contact with Francona's so the manager could sense the sincerity. "Never."

And soon they were off to Birmingham, beginning one of the most enchanting tales in American sports history. The country's most popular athlete, who earned $30 million in endorsements alone, had accepted a job that paid $850 a month. He spent his time on a 45-foot luxury bus, "luxury" because in the words of Francona, "It didn't break down much and it didn't stink; it actually looked like the Partridge Family bus." That garish green-and-purple bus was where you could find a bunch of kids happy to make $10,000 a year, sitting next to the handsome spokesman for Nike, Gatorade, and Coca-Cola.

It was as if the companies were satisfied with Jordan's performance in all the top 25 markets, so they wanted to know how he'd go over in the flesh somewhere between Tupelo, Mississippi, and Talladega, Alabama. It was one thing to see Jordan go to McDonald's in his commercials, but it was quite another to see him there at 3:00 A.M., ordering fries on his way to Orlando, Jacksonville, and Greenville, North Carolina.

Extended travel is one of the great tests of any relationship, especially the trips in which the 5-hour mark means that you're only halfway there. Jordan had been used to traveling on private jets and chartered flights, but he enjoyed the bus hours because that was the time when he could not be reached. He could let his guard down and not worry about being the guy America knew from 48-minute games and 60-second jingles. Sometimes that meant going to the back of the bus and playing dominoes with the kids, and at times it was edging toward the front and listening in on the conversations of the coaches, who were all close to his age. They saw the things that made him one of the guys, like how he ate where they ate and stayed where they stayed. They also saw flashes of his former life, flashes of how he reached the point where people just said *Michael* and you knew who they meant.

Forget about the great start he was able to have at the plate, hitting .330 in late April. He did have a background in basketball, right? The coaches were reminded of that one day on the bus when they mentioned a pickup game they planned to play in Birmingham. Jordan wasn't listening to their conversation. At least, he wasn't in the beginning. But the more they talked about playing, the more he rubbed those huge palms of his together. After a while, it became clear that inviting him to play was moot. He was going to play when they got back to Birmingham whether they wanted him to or not.

The game was a treat for anyone who happened to be walking near the public court where some locals, some Barons, Francona, and Jordan were playing. Word spread quickly that Michael Jordan—*the* Michael Jordan—was playing ball at the park. The only thing that distinguished him at first was his height. He was playing an understated game, getting everyone else involved, and graciously passing the ball even though anyone playing or watching knew what he was capable of doing. One of the young locals, tall and ripped, a twentyish athlete, didn't seem convinced. There's always someone who wants to show a superstar that they don't believe everything they see on TV.

Birmingham had that someone, aggressively talking trash to Jordan.

Francona was nervous. He didn't like that a large crowd had gathered, and he wasn't comfortable with the tone of the game. It had started out small, but now they had a block party, an audience split between admirers and instigators. What kind of explanation would he have for Reinsdorf and general manager Ron Schueler if he had to tell them that Jordan had been hurt during a basketball game? What would they say in Chicago: Jordan can't play for the Bulls, but he can find time to school some wannabe in a public park?

The manager didn't have to worry long. For 30 seconds, the public court became Chicago Stadium or Madison Square Garden, and the young mouth became another in a line of kids who needed to be taught a lesson the hard and high way. Jordan made sure the defending kid was close enough to be taken for a harsh ride. The journey began just inside the free-throw line and it ended in a rapid and angry blur: the kid jumped, Jordan jumped higher, the ball was slammed through the rim hard enough to instantly bend it, and the kid was on the ground with Jordan standing over him.

"Don't ever talk shit to me on *my* court," he shouted.

Game over, and a public court in Birmingham claimed as his own.

His teammates and coaches probably saw the most complete portrait of Jordan in 1994. They saw the public figure, just like everyone else. They saw the competitor who destroyed tennis rackets and Ping-Pong tables after losses. They saw the self-assured Michael, watching his former team play the Knicks on TV and turning to Francona to say, "I don't think they can win this game. They don't have the guy they need right now." Meaning himself. They all had inside information if they wanted to take advantage of it—and they didn't—about one of the reasons he retired from the NBA: he was bored with the paint-by-numbers routine, even though you had to be supremely gifted to say that "showing up and getting my 30 points" was part of the monotony.

The most shocking thing they saw, though, was his occasional shyness and embarrassment. He didn't impose his will so easily on baseball. His .330 average in April had dipped about 100 points, to .234, going into the long Memorial Day weekend. The Chicago dailies kept a "Jordan Watch," with each sliding stat encouraging everyone that he would be back with the Bulls the next season. Even as he struggled, Francona saw some of his athletic and diplomatic strengths.

The manager was amazed that Jordan couldn't get down a bunt during batting practice, but when the Barons needed it in a game, he would lay down a gem. Each of his 436 at bats during the season was somebody else's moment to be a star, so he didn't get the benefit of a lot of mistakes. Or fastballs. They threw him sliders and curves, and he swung and missed more than anyone on the team. He was the attraction of the league, even though he didn't feel comfortable getting the attention given his struggles. He admired his teammates, not just for the ability to play baseball, but for all the hard work that was rewarded with scant cash. Flaunting his riches was something they never saw him do.

Francona's mission as a manager was to put all his players in a position to think about playing and nothing else. So he learned to tiptoe around the desires of management—they didn't want one of Jordan's bodyguards, George Koehler, in the dugout—and do what was best for the team, which was to give Koehler an all-access pass. It made everyone's job easier. Francona was a young manager, but he was already displaying a gift for understanding the needs of ownership, the media, and his team, and working it so that one didn't pull from the other.

Not many people knew that White Sox management did not allow him to bat Jordan ninth, despite an average that leveled off between the high .180s and low .200s. They also would flip if he or anyone else in the organization used the word "circus" to describe Jordan's year in baseball. Francona once got a voice mail from Chicago, blasting him for using the word "circus" to the Birmingham media. (It turns out that they were misinformed and he hadn't used the word.) They were extremely sensitive to the public perception of what Jordan was doing, and they didn't want anyone on staff to come close to repeating any of the sentiments that were in the media.

Francona was good at getting to know his players, learning what motivated them, bringing them together, and then protecting them. He kept them from the *circus* of front-office politics because it got in the way of playing. He also gained everyone's trust because he was more concerned with getting things right privately than looking good publicly. He protected Jordan the same way he protected his young players; the difference was that Jordan received requests that other players didn't.

Once, in Jacksonville, the GM of their team wanted to make a big deal of presenting Jordan with the key to the city. He approached Jordan, and the Barons' famous left fielder declined. The GM persisted and Jordan declined again. He was hitting .180-something and he didn't think it was the right time. Finally, Francona intervened.

"Sir, he's been really nice," he said. "Can't you see he's embarrassed? He just doesn't want to do it."

A screaming match between Francona and the GM ensued in Francona's office. The door had been closed, but Jordan opened it and threatened the GM: "If you don't knock it off, I'm going to own your team. And he's going to be running it." He was pointing to Francona. The dispute was over, and the next day Francona had a no-hard-feelings gift—a golden cigar cutter—waiting on his desk.

As poor as Jordan's hitting was, few people outside of Birmingham seemed to grasp how much fun he was having joking around with the players and coaching staff. He also was playful with the national and Chicago media, members of whom would drop in on the Southern League and see how Jordan was doing. He understood that many of them were waiting for a made-for-TV confession—Oprah Winfrey/Barbara Walters–style—in which he would give an exclusive and give up baseball in one sitting.

He teased, knowingly, but he wasn't biting. Lacy J. Banks of the *Sun-Times* visited in July, and Jordan openly played with his mind in a question-and-answer column.

JORDAN: I'm never coming back to play basketball. Not in this
   lifetime.
BANKS: Never?
JORDAN: Never . . . Unless I change my mind.

Later, on the way out, Jordan did more intentional spinning.

BANKS: I just want to make this thing clear now as we end this
   interview. You say that in this lifetime you will never play
   basketball again?

JORDAN: I'm going to give it to you plain and simple. I'm not, in the near future or in the age that I am living, planning on playing professional basketball again . . . unless I change my mind.

They also didn't understand that the humble minor league life was what Jordan needed and wanted. It was his respite from the constant hero worship. He liked it when he scorched his teammates and they gave it right back to him. He would never be viewed as normal, given who he was, but the minors got him as close to normal as he had been in years. Unfortunately, normal in some Southern circles wasn't all pleasant.

Since Francona and Jordan loved to golf for money—Francona routinely shot in the 70s, so he had a slightly higher winning percentage—they would compete whenever they got the chance. Francona's bets were much more conservative than the star's. The manager's entire salary, $32,000, was roughly the amount of fines Jordan gladly paid for skipping out on a few media sessions during the NBA's All-Star weekends. With Jordan, the size of the bet was secondary to the rush of competition; he'd be as excited to win $50 as $5,000, especially if there was some type of comeback or pressure shot involved.

One of their golf outings was at Shoal Creek Country Club, where they sat in the dining room and caused a stir. Two white men spoke loudly of being in "certain" company, and made a production out of getting up and leaving. Jordan played it cool and kept talking with Francona. After a long pause, Francona spoke.

"That was terrible," he said to Jordan. "I wasn't sure what to do."

"You did well," Jordan answered. "That's the way you should have handled it."

It was a surprise and it wasn't. Both of them had tried to prepare for incidents that could quickly become inflamed, and that was one of the reasons Francona allowed Koehler to go wherever he wanted. Koehler had a knack for scoping out potential issues before they became problematic, so Francona considered him to be a valuable member of the Barons. It was also one of the reasons Jordan had insisted on a reliable bus. He and the team would be traveling late nights and early mornings through parts of the South where, frankly, they didn't give a damn about Jordan's ads or his skills or his famous smile. They didn't want to see him or anyone who looked like him.

For the most part, Jordan's issues in Birmingham were on the field. Francona believed that if Jordan had the benefit of 2,000 at bats in the minors—or 4 years—he'd have found a spot in the majors, even if that role was defensive replacement or pinch runner. But even his most optimistic supporter didn't envision a 4-year stay in the minors. In fact, those who got a chance to see him play each Sunday in the Arizona Fall League, as Francona did, wondered, "Why not the Bulls?"

After Jordan's season in Birmingham ended with a .202 average, 51 runs batted in, and 30 stolen bases, it was time for Francona and Jordan to head to the Fall League's Scottsdale Scorpions. When they weren't playing short-season baseball, a lot of the players and coaches would have their pickup basketball games. The environment was the opposite of the park in Birmingham: private and controlled. Jordan's role on the court, though, was unchanged. He would take over if he needed to, but he was there more for the workout and to set up his teammates.

They played three or four full-court games to 11 by 1's. In the final game, Francona took a long jump shot that missed, and the long rebound went to Curtis Pride. He dribbled a few times, went to the air, and slammed in the winning points. Francona was relieved. He had been tired of playing anyway. Good for Curtis. He heard a ball hit the backboard, as if someone had thrown it there, and he knew Jordan was walking fast behind him.

"Hey," the star said as he caught up with him. "I always shoot last."

"I know you do on TV," Francona shot back.

"Seriously, I don't give a shit where we are. I always shoot last."

He walked ahead of Francona now. It was that fast pace he had in the NBA when he was furiously chewing gum, stewing about an official's call, and plotting his next game-changing flurry to make everything all right. He stopped in his tracks to kneel down and laugh when he heard Francona quip, "Now you know how I feel when you try to hit a curveball."

The truth was that Jordan was getting better, hitting .260 in the Fall League. He had learned a lot more about baseball, too, much different than the player who had once stolen a base with the Barons up by 11 runs. ("Hey, if they're going to give me a layup . . .") Francona was more convinced than ever that managing a team of stars would not be a problem if one or two of those stars had the personality of Jordan. In that case, the manager-as-tyrant would be redundant because clubhouse policy would be set by the manager and enforced by alpha personalities like Jordan. Could it work in baseball? Definitely; Jordan himself made it work in baseball and he was new to the sport.

The key was to have players who could command the respect of their teammates, and to have a manager secure enough to accept input from those players. Jordan showed Francona that he clearly got it one day in Scottsdale. Francona told Jordan ahead of time that he was going to have a day game off following a night game. It was perfect timing for Jordan because a few of his boys were in town, and Jordan wasn't known for quiet evenings and lights out by 10:30. He had a good time that night and it showed: he arrived for the day game on time, but he was leaning on the dugout rail with his sunglasses on. Thank God for off days.

But there was a change of plans.

Francona had allowed one of the outfielders to go home to attend a wedding, and he absolutely had to pull Michael Tucker from a game because Tucker wasn't doing what he was supposed to on the base paths. Francona was coaching third and gave a shrug to Jordan, as in, "I know I gave you the day off, but I need you." Jordan took off the glasses, slowly grabbed a bat, and began to get loose. He worked the pitcher for a walk and then barreled into second base with an emphatic, head-first slide.

Francona asked him why he was sliding like that into second. "I know why you took Tucker out," he answered. "He wasn't going hard into second. That'll show him how it's done."

Jordan was all about lessons and competition. He thrived on them, usually because he was on the giving end of the former and the winning end of the latter. It didn't matter if he was inviting Francona to play golf with him, Charles Barkley, Vince Coleman, and Roy Green, or if it was just the two of them playing together. He was the same: he treated people well, regardless of their position. But his competitiveness was consistent, so he had no mercy on you—regardless of your position—if you challenged him and lost.

A kid club pro at the beachfront Sawgrass Country Club, just outside of Jacksonville, learned this when he told Jordan that he didn't think he could sink a 30-foot putt. Francona shook his head and thought of his standard line about Jordan: "When you tell him no, the answer is usually 'yes.'" Jordan was intrigued. He had another one on the hook, ready to reel him in. "Well, I need some odds," he said.

How many times had Francona seen this? It was amazing to see an elite athlete zone in on something that was outside of his sport of expertise. Even if the goal is not met, there is something fascinating about watching the high effort and concentration. In this case, Francona just knew that the club pro was going to be losing money that he didn't have. The kid had underestimated Jordan. The bet was $50, the odds were 4 to 1. There wasn't much wasted time before the ball was in the hole. The kid was ashen; he clearly didn't have the money on him.

"I'm not going to take your money," Jordan said. "But this is what you're going to do: I saw two silk golf shirts I liked in the pro shop. They're one hundred dollars apiece. Go pick those up for me."

Jordan's competitive light was always on, and these small victories in anonymity were fun, but they were not satisfying. They were refreshing. He needed stakes, a stage, critics, drama. He was the best basketball player in the world, so he was going to return to being an NBA star and champion. For Francona, all he needed was a good opportunity. When he got it, he'd become a champion, flawlessly managing the stars.

CHAPTER 6

Yankee Chess

Two hours was about all he could handle. Two hours of sleep—one hour for each of the previous night's games—and it was time to wake up and do something. Anything. Terry Francona couldn't sit still, even if he had told himself that he would.

His two youngest daughters, Leah and Jamie, were downstairs. For them and everyone else in the Franconas' Chestnut Hill house, it was a lovely Saturday morning, August 19, 2006. For him, who knows, it could have still been Friday night at Fenway. He could have been in the seventh inning of either loss to the Yankees, sweating and rocking in his dugout seat. His nerves were jumping again, as they had before the five-game series started, because he knew it was a bad time for the Yankees to be in town. The teams were separated by two games in the American League East standings when the series began, and two games in, the Red Sox were already slipping.

It's the strangest thing: you can go outside the morning after a game against the Yankees and feel what happened the night before. It's as if all of Boston is a weathervane, pointing in the general direction of the Red Sox. On this summer day, it was a straight shot to the south. The Yankees had swept the doubleheader, 12 to 4 and 14 to 11. Their lead in the division was three and a half games. It was being written about in the papers, talked about on the radio, rehashed and agonized over in checkout lines.

That's how it works with Yankees–Red Sox, which has the DNA of a high school rivalry and the cash of Wells Fargo. Each team makes a move with the other one in mind, so every meeting during the season is an unofficial poll to see which team is superior. Overreaction and pettiness are to be expected. It happens year after year, and the fact that the Red Sox won the World Series in 2004 didn't quiet the competition; it intensified it.

Since 2004, Francona's first season with the team, he had become more knowledgeable about the city and what makes it tick. In the beginning, he may have believed the post–World Series fantasy peddled by outsiders: things would be kinder and gentler in Boston once the angst of not winning for so long was taken away. There was happiness over winning, but it didn't mean that the manager was suddenly elevated to hero status and couldn't be second-guessed. No Red Sox manager will ever be an unquestioned hero. It's New England baseball, the ongoing dialogue, so there are thousands of at-home managers out there, convinced that they would do this or that differently and better. And it's like that when the Red Sox are winning.

There are many days when Francona goes to the office and finds e-mails telling him what a terrible manager he is for, you name it, taking a pitcher out too early or leaving him in too long. There are days when he turns on the radio and hears that old insult from Philadelphia: "Fran*coma!* I'm telling ya, this guy should be fired . . ." He's not shaken by the criticism, not just because he feels that it's a natural flip side to passion, but because his handling of the criticism is one thing that heightens his credibility and trust with his players. He won't crack publicly, no matter how rough a slump, so they know he'll never try to make himself look good at their expense.

The more time Francona spent in Boston, the more he understood Red Sox–Yankees. It was exhausting and nerve-racking. It was fans reacting to each pitch, each throw over to first, and each managerial move. Francona felt the Northeastern frenzy the first time he managed in a Red Sox–Yankees game. He was so energized by the atmosphere that he talked to himself in the dugout: "Come on, you big dumbass, take a seat and relax."

He was going to need a similar pep talk on this Saturday morning, working on two hours' sleep. He left the house, drove to Starbucks for the usual, egg salad sandwich and a large coffee—and headed to Fenway. Who cares if you talk with your mouth full when you're alone? He had that talk as he ate the sandwich. There was no way he could go into the clubhouse and let anyone see last night's losses still showing on his face. He had talked so much about not letting the losses linger for days and weeks, he had to live up to his words. After he arrived at the park, he went straight to the weight room to lift and run away the stress.

The season was becoming a mess.

The Red Sox had been on pace for 100 victories, and then they started to break down in July. Jason Varitek got hurt on the last day of the month, the day of the trading deadline, and the team was forced to acquire a catcher, Javy Lopez, whom they didn't want. They hadn't received favorable reports on his personality, and they didn't think he would be a good fit for the team. They were right, he wasn't ideal for them, but they didn't have a lot of choices. Pitcher Tim Wakefield got hurt two weeks before Varitek, and no one knew when the knuckleballer would be ready again. Manny Ramirez, supremely talented and maddeningly unpredictable, was having a great season. But . . . you never know with Manny. Sometimes he'll give you a look, which means it's probably time to give him a day off. Sometimes it's better to give Manny a rest before he takes one on his own.

It was getting to the point where no one was capable of running into the manager's office and surprising him by blurting out, "You won't believe what just happened . . ." Yes, he would believe it. Whatever it was, it was plausible. It was quickly turning into that kind of year. So it wasn't enough that the Red Sox would lose their Saturday-afternoon game 13 to 5. Or that they had given up 39 runs in the previous 24 hours. The surprise of the day was starting pitcher Josh Beckett, who packed nine earned runs, nine walks, and 121 pitches into five and two-thirds innings. Beckett's season ERA was approaching the mid-fives, meaning that he was slumping at the same time one of the players for whom he was traded, Hanley Ramirez, was making his push to be the National League's Rookie of the Year.

After that game, with the Red Sox now four and a half games back, Francona was convinced that he was going to be in the paper. Not just him, but the coaching staff, baseball operations, ownership, everybody. It just happened to be the weekend that John Henry, the team's principal owner, had long planned to throw Theo Epstein an engagement party. The party was on Henry's boat, which was docked in Boston Harbor. They had lost three consecutive games to the Yankees and now they were having a party on the water. Francona didn't major in journalism at the University of Arizona, but he knew enough about New York tabloids and Boston dailies to understand that they would have fun if they ever got hold of a picture. What would the irreverent headline writers at the *New York Post* do with this one?

Boston Flee Party?

Three Sheets to the Wind?

They never got that picture, but any analogy connected to sinking still fit. There were two more games and two more losses, both contributing to the rare final total for the Yankees: a five-game sweep. It's something that doesn't happen to good teams, and certainly not at home. The Yankees had won the latest leg of the high school competition, valedictorians for the weekend, while the Red Sox—in the front office—were already thinking about how to beat the Yankees in the off-season.

As embarrassing as the losses on the field had been, the news away from the games was much more important and serious. In late August and the first week of September, the following happened to Red Sox players:

- Jon Lester, a 22-year-old rookie pitcher, was diagnosed with non-Hodgkin's lymphoma, a treatable blood cancer;
- David Ortiz, the team's leading home run hitter and run producer, was hospitalized with heart palpitations;
- Ramirez, who had taken himself out of the fifth game of the Yankees series with a sore hamstring, played just 10 more games the remainder of the season. His official injury, according to the team, was patellar tendinitis;
- Curt Schilling, the team's most productive starting pitcher, missed 3 weeks with a muscle strain;
- Jonathan Papelbon, the dominant rookie closer with the sub-1.00 ERA, walked off the mound holding and shaking his right arm. Later, he was diagnosed with a shoulder subluxation, which meant his shoulder had slipped forward slightly, away from its socket.

For the Red Sox, the 2006 season had become about prayer sessions, not playoff pushes. They weren't going to catch the Yankees, and they didn't have enough healthy players to make a wild-card run. On the day that the team lost its fourth straight game to New York, Epstein talked with reporters on the field. A kid who grows up in Boston and then goes on to become the GM of the Red Sox understands the mentality when things go wrong in August, especially if they go wrong against the Yankees. There has to be a reason for the team being engulfed in flames, and the reason can't be too civil (i.e., "They've got good players, too") or too abstract. Some years it's the players, often it's the manager, and in 2006 it was Epstein. He was receiving most of his criticism for not making a move at the trading deadline. The names most often mentioned were Bobby Abreu, who went to the Yankees, and Roy Oswalt, the Houston pitcher whose name had been floated in a trade before he re-signed with the Astros.

Asked why the team didn't go after Abreu, who would have been costly, Epstein said, "We have tremendous resources, don't get me wrong. But that's not something we can do. We have a plan. We're in a position competing with less resources [than the Yankees]." Epstein did have a plan, and part of his plan may have begun with that quote. The Yankees really weren't going to fall for the sympathetic public service announcement, were they? The only thing missing was, *Please, you can make a difference: no amount donated is too small* . . .

No team generates income like the Yankees, but the Red Sox have a high-profit cable TV network and the richest radio deal in baseball. They'd be all right. By the time Epstein told a truth that couldn't have been more correct, his listeners had reached shutdown mode, believing that they had come to the corporate-speak section of the interview. If they had been in a boardroom rather than on a baseball field, they would have started to draw stick figures in the margins of their legal notebooks and jotted down players they wanted to draft for their fantasy football teams.

"There's a lot of great development that's gone on this year," Epstein said to symbolic eye rolls. "And I think it will bode well for the future."

What he didn't mention was that some of the development had taken place in Rhode Island and Maine, where Dustin Pedroia and Jacoby Ellsbury were lunching on minor league pitching. Epstein was high on both of them, and he was counting on Pedroia to be his starter at second base in 2007. But no one wants to hear about next year in August, following a Yankee sweep. And when Pedroia did make his big-league debut a couple days later, he didn't appear to be anything special. He was barely 5 feet 8 inches, he had the swing of a man a foot taller, and he finished the season with an average of .191. Then again, it wasn't fair to judge anyone, kid callups included, on the way they looked at the end of the season. The Red Sox won 86 games, a low total by New York–Boston standards, and limped to the finish 11 games behind the Yankees.

The Yankees went on to the postseason, installed as favorites against the Detroit Tigers, and lost the first-round series in four games. Since Detroit was the American League's representative in the World Series, it would be natural for all teams to measure themselves against them. Not in Boston. Not in New York. Even when neither of them won, they were still occupied with each other.

The good thing about the competitive obsession between the Yankees and Red Sox is that the obsession often leads to self-criticism, which leads to action. When the Red Sox were embarrassed in the Grady Game, for all of New York and America to see, it led to an aggressive off-season in which Francona was hired,

Schilling and closer Keith Foulke were acquired, Ramirez was placed on waivers—remarkably, there were no takers—and Alex Rodriguez was pursued. Maybe Epstein had the information in his back pocket the entire time he was doing his interview with the reporters; maybe he knew then that he would be authorized by ownership to push the budget envelope if he thought a player was worth it.

He had some names in mind, of course, but first he had to play out free agency inside the Red Sox offices. Having magnetic strips with the names of free agents on a big board was not good enough. Not this year. He wanted to be certain that he and his staff understood the free agency landscape, globally and in the States, better than anyone else in baseball. So he went to members of baseball operations like vice president Ben Cherington and assistant general manager Jed Hoyer, vice president of international scouting Craig Shipley, and director of baseball operations Brian O'Halloran. There were about 20 employees, all of them assigned teams and agents to "represent" in a simulation. One of them would be superagent Scott Boras, others would be GMs such as the Yankees' Brian Cashman, White Sox's Ken Williams, Mets' Omar Minaya, Giants' Brian Sabean, Angels' Bill Stoneman . . . all of them were at Fenway to give the Red Sox a sneak preview of what might happen once free agent contracts were extended.

They all spent several days studying the needs and financial restrictions of their teams-for-the-week. Once they began competing for players in their virtual baseball world, they saw just how thin pitching was, and that teams desperate for pitching actually did have the resources to acquire it. They predicted free-agent pitcher Barry Zito's 7-year, $126 million contract to the letter. They were dead-on with Gil Meche, the former Mariners pitcher who signed a $55 million contract in Kansas City. They were within 5 percent of most of the real contracts, which sounds like good news, but what it told them was that they had a lot of competition for the pitcher they really wanted.

His name was Daisuke Matsuzaka, and they had been studying him for years. Shipley and Pacific Rim scout Jon Deeble had seen him pitch in Japan for the Seibu Lions. He would be perfect for the Red Sox; how often do you get the chance to sign a 26-year-old pitcher with star potential for reasonable dollars? They had heard how smart and durable Matsuzaka was, but that's not the report that most got their attention. They were hearing that Matsuzaka was so eager to pitch in the States that if he had been able, he'd have done it for $3 million a year. They knew that wasn't going to happen, not with Boras—the real one or the one in role-play—representing him. The point was that they could be dynamic and *needed* to be dynamic in their bid for the pitcher.

The bidding, or posting, process is the lifeblood of conspiracy theorists. Each team interested in a player must submit its post to Major League Baseball, and then the information is passed on to the team who holds the player's rights. A winner is announced, and that team has a month to sign the player to a deal. If you were raised on James Bond or even Jason Bourne, you can see loopholes in the process. You imagine submitting your bid 15 minutes before the deadline, and then having a secret source drop a dime to the competition, trumping your bid. You imagine prearranged deals between Japanese teams and teams in the States, complete with insider information of what it will really take for a player to sign.

Epstein and the Red Sox believed in the system; they just didn't want to take any chances with it. If they believed in their people who were scouting Asia, then their plan was obvious: bid high, outrageously high if necessary, and then sign low. They waited until 1 minute before the deadline to submit their record-shattering number, $51.1 million, to Major League Baseball. Just like in the movies, they had "a man on the scene"—O'Halloran was at the MLB offices in New York—to make sure the operation went smoothly.

Fifty-one million dollars was risky. Fifty-one million dollars was a lot of money for a team without the New York Yankees' resources, wink-wink. The Red Sox paid *$51 million dollars,* due all at once, for the right to negotiate with a pitcher who had never done anything in the majors. Even if the words on the street were true and the Red Sox could sign Matsuzaka for as little as $3 million a season for six seasons, that would be at least $70 million devoted to an unknown in the American game. Realistically, the Red Sox knew the per-season average would fall somewhere between $7 million and $9 million, pushing the deal over $100 million. This is what usually happens in baseball or any other business when you guess wrong on a $100 million investment:

You get fired.

Epstein briefly left the Red Sox, on his own accord, in the fall of 2005. In the winter of 2006, he was giving ownership a gaudy paper trail with which to work, just in case some of his chances didn't work out. For a while, it seemed that Epstein was the only one in Boston excited about the opportunity to sign former Dodgers outfielder J.D. Drew. In early November, Drew opted out of a contract that guaranteed him $33 million in its final 3 years. New England wasn't the only region of the country where fans wondered where Drew, coming off a 20-home run, 100-RBI season, would match what he left in Los Angeles. Not only did Epstein plan to match it, he was going to exceed it. The public had come to know Drew as a talented player who displayed almost no passion. He was a quiet craftsman who showed up at work, often read a book while his teammates were clowning around, did his job, and went home. His talent was as undeniable as his injury history.

When there were reports that the Red Sox were locked in on signing Drew to a salary averaging $14 million per season, the move, and Drew, was booed before it was official. Epstein held a conference call with local reporters in late November to give an update on the team. His mind was clearly on signing Matsuzaka, but there were Red Sox employees he wouldn't talk to about that; there was no chance he'd be specific with the media. He spent his time doing the executive waltz, lots of pauses, hesitations, and half-turns. He really didn't say much, and that led to a humorous exchange with *Boston Globe* columnist Bob Ryan.

> RYAN (exasperated, breathless): What's the fascination, if true, with J.D. Drew?
>
> EPSTEIN (probably checking his BlackBerry): Uh, you know, Bob, I don't think it's appropriate to talk about potential free-agent signings . . .
>
> RYAN (dramatic gasp): What are we going to accomplish today then, Theo?
>
> EPSTEIN (probably reading from a memo): I was asked by your colleagues to be made available as regularly as possible during the off-season . . .
>
> RYAN (pleading): On behalf of an eager constituency, let's hope that the rumor is not true. Thank you.

It was true. Epstein had heard about the lack of passion, the lack of durability, the meticulous discipline—some called it "passivity"—

at the plate. What he saw was a player who could be perfectly slotted behind the left-handed Ortiz and right-handed Ramirez, giving Francona the left-right-left lineup construction that made it difficult for opposing managers to match up with the Red Sox late in games.

As for Francona, he knew Epstein well enough to understand that when the GM was quiet, he was probably working on something big. Epstein gave Francona general updates on what he was doing to sign Matsuzaka, but he didn't get into all the specifics. To this day, he says, "We did some stuff out in Orange County [where Boras's office is] that will never come out until I write my book. It was some exciting stuff—like the movie *No Way Out*. I can't tell you about it, but I think that was the most fun I've ever had in baseball."

Before the 48 hours of excitement that preceded the signing of Matsuzaka, Francona and Epstein were among many Red Sox employees who had dinner with the pitcher at the California home of Tom Werner, one of the Red Sox's owners. They never discussed money. It was an introductory meeting, one in which it was obvious to Francona that his biggest challenge in 2007 would be getting Matsuzaka to just relax around him. The player-manager relationship in Japan is nothing like the relationship in the States. You don't joke with the manager and talk with him casually.

Sensing the pitcher's discomfort, Francona tried to put him at ease: "A few months from now, you'll be sitting on my couch with your feet up on my desk."

Boras disagreed. "I don't think so," the agent said. "That will not be happening."

The 2007 team was beginning to take shape before New Year's Day. The Red Sox added Matsuzaka and reliever Hideki

Okajima from Japan. They got Drew and shortstop Julio Lugo, also a former Dodger, in free agency. They gave the job at second to Pedroia. Once they got to spring training in Fort Myers, Florida, all they had to do was wait to see when Ramirez would arrive.

Ramirez is always a story in the spring, for the organization and for the writers who cover him. The writers have the easier job: all they have to do is report when he arrives. For Francona and Epstein, February and March are months of diplomacy. The previous season might have ended with a Ramirez trade request or a controversial injury. Whatever the case, that story is inevitably continued in the spring, and it becomes exacerbated if, by chance, Ramirez is not in attendance with the rest of his teammates.

In February, the story was complicated. Teammate Julian Tavarez said he spoke with Ramirez, and reported that his teammate would be in camp on March 1. The reason, Tavarez said, was that Ramirez was in the Miami area, caring for his sick mother. The problem was that Tavarez had heard the news before Epstein and Francona had.

Managing the slugger is one of the easiest and most trying things a manager can experience. Ramirez is the type of player that Dick Williams had in mind when he said that he was not fit for dealing with today's game. Back in the day, "losing" a player meant that he was gone if he didn't do what you asked. Today, losing a player means that you have to ease into issues and problems, lest you spin a player into a sulking session that could last multiple games. Ramirez's ability to hit a baseball is downright seductive. There isn't a pitch he can't hit, a field he can't reach, a great closer or relief specialist upon whom he can't inflict self-doubt.

In Boston, where he rarely speaks with the media, he is either described as a harmless clubhouse eccentric or a distraction. He is neither; what he is, from a managerial perspective, is a player who requires explanation and elaboration. Francona knows that his players are not at all offended by Ramirez, but they do deserve some background when they hear, for example, that he is arriving after them for spring training.

From the first day he managed Michael Jordan to the first day he met Ortiz and Varitek, Francona championed a democratic philosophy of management. He believed that conscientious players who could command a room—Jordan, Ortiz, Varitek—had the right to help shape policy. After all, it was their team, too. If the players were as intensely devoted to championships as he was, then Francona was confident that they had the same agenda: winning as many games as possible. He gained their trust with his knowledge of baseball, yes, but also with his willingness to give them insight into his thinking.

He called the team together in spring training, with Ramirez still not there, and allowed everyone to speak for 45 minutes. He explained the situation to them and told them that he would do whatever the majority decided was right. But, he added, he wanted to make everyone aware of the consequences. This wasn't as simple as some of the draconian solutions mentioned in office break rooms and Internet chat rooms; you can't ignore everything that Ramirez does "as long as he hits," just as you can't banish him to the bench or a corner until "he does what you say."

It's not that Francona told his players something they didn't know. They were simply appreciative of the gesture. Much more so than his first year, when they weren't sure what to make of him and he was getting used to them, he now had a room filled with reliable assistant principals capable of enforcing policy. Not that policy was tangled up in dozens of rules (music is the big one: headphones have to be used on the plane, and that day's starter gets to choose the music for the clubhouse; any complaints lead to a no-music zone). Just as he could with Jordan, who wasn't the best player in Double-A, Francona knew that he could go to Ortiz and say, "This is the problem," and he would have to say no more. Big Papi would fix it and further assure the manager with a "No problem, bro." In the middle of the Yankees series that ended the Red Sox's 2006 season, it was Ortiz who stopped in the manager's office with a couple of Presidente beers from the Dominican Republic. Francona had players with various styles of conflict resolution available if he needed help with Ramirez. Alex Cora could talk calmly, Varitek could just give a look, and Ortiz was the ultimate bridge-builder.

Once, Francona was so frustrated with Ramirez that he told Ortiz, "I'm going to kill him." Ortiz listened and told the manager that he'd check on Ramirez. After a while, Ortiz returned with a smile and a statement: "It's all right for you to kill him now." The big man had the perfect personality and presence for dealing with a variety of issues.

After all the talking about Ramirez, he showed up on March 1, so he wasn't even the big story of the spring. Instead, in what seemed like a page out of 2003, the Red Sox were hoping that someone could take Papelbon's closer job. The team's medical staff had indicated that the best way to keep Papelbon's shoulder strong was to put him on a throwing program consistent with a starter's. Epstein was intrigued with the idea of having someone with Papelbon's repertoire in the rotation for 200 innings. He thought someone from the group of Joel Pineiro, Brendan Donnelly, Mike Timlin, or maybe even Okajima could close.

It sounded okay, except for one small thing: Papelbon wasn't okay with it. He was talking with Varitek one day, and he let it be known that he missed closing. His two best pitches, a fastball and splitter, were made for the role. A starter with that combination might run into trouble in the fifth or sixth inning, if that's all he has. But you're not worried about the fifth when you're closing. A fastball in the high 90s, one that can turn a catcher's good leather into distressed leather, is enough to do the job. Adding a splitter is enough to elevate the closer to unhittable status.

Papelbon talked to Varitek, Varitek talked to Francona and pitching coach John Farrell, the two of them talked with Epstein, and everybody spoke with the doctors. Once they were clear on a program that would allow Papelbon to close without damaging his shoulder, the move was made. Papelbon's story was the team's story, in that the only obstacle blocking greatness was health.

In mid-March 2007, Francona got a visit from a man who could talk to him about greatness, staying healthy, and the risks of spending big in free agency. At Mark Shapiro's insistence, Scott Pioli and Francona had met. The GM of the Indians considers Pioli one of his best friends, and from what he knew of Francona's personality—Shapiro hired him as an adviser in 2001—he thought the two would get along well. He was right. A few years before, they had sat at the same table for a function in Boston, the Italian-American Hall of Fame, and they couldn't stop with the laughs and one-liners. Since Francona is a huge football fan, he loved any opportunity he could get to pick the brain of Pioli, the New England Patriots' leading personnel man during their championship run.

On the March day Pioli visited, Francona stood near him wearing a huge grin. It's not that Pioli was saying something funny; he was talking with agent Drew Rosenhaus and finalizing the fine points of receiver Donte Stallworth's contract. The manager admired the Patriots and couldn't get enough stories about their coaching philosophy as well as their draft approach. The two of them found that there were some similarities in their industries, and in some cases—from disciplining players to what type of gamesmanship was considered crossing the line—their cultures clashed. But the interest in player evaluation made sense for Francona: few people outside of Shapiro and some Red Sox insiders know the depths of the manager's skills as an evaluator.

He was one of the first people in the organization who said he thought Papelbon should be a closer. Papelbon was being groomed as a starter then, and he was a completely different pitcher: he was a little chubbier, and he was mixing an average slider and curveball with his astonishing fastball and splitter. Francona watched the way he handled himself in a spring training game against the Orioles, following a questionable brushback pitch from temperamental starter Daniel Cabrera. On his own, Papelbon put some heat near the chin of Sammy Sosa, and kept his composure by working his way out of the inning. Francona never forgot the incident, and always thought the organization's prized pitcher could one day become the best closer in the game.

Francona and his team were going to head back to Boston with Papelbon filling the spot that he had vacated in September. There had been a lot of guessing and speculating about the Red Sox and Yankees and which team, in 2007, was better. Neither team had to wait long to see how the other had managed to tighten and tweak itself since the September sweep.

Fourteen games into the season, the Red Sox and Yankees were scheduled to meet for a three-game series at Fenway. The Red Sox were 9 and 5; the Yankees were 8 and 6. And so it all returned. The nerves, the pacing, the energy: all there. Across from Francona, amazingly, was the same man who used to watch him take candy from the Atlanta Braves clubhouse in the 1960s.

Joe Torre was a player then, in his late 20s, just being nice to Tito's boy, Little Tito. Now there was Torre, in his 60s, managing the Yankees and trying to do everything possible so his team could crush Little Tito's.

They did this two dozen times a year, if they met in the playoffs, and the strategy never got old.

Francona has a system for these games and all the others. It usually begins the night before a game or first thing in the morning, when no players are around. He hates the thought of them coming into the clubhouse needing him, and him off somewhere doing work that could have been done earlier.

He starts with the reports from the advance scouts. He sifts through the comments and numbers and then makes himself a loaded, and succinct, scouting report to carry with him in the dugout. His system is color-coded: green means that the matchup is excellent for the Red Sox (Derek Jeter and Johnny Damon were a combined 6 for 47 against Mike Timlin going into the series); red means that there is danger for the Red Sox (Robinson Cano was 3 for 5 against Timlin); black is used for either basic information or notes.

On the left side of his reports, Francona has the team's stolen-base stats. On the right side, he leaves spaces for pithy or abbreviated comments:

"Jeter: slightly weaker vs. rh . . . Giambi: struggling vs. rh (normally weaker vs. lh) . . . Posada: swinging very well vs. lh now . . . Cabrera: struggling vs. both sides . . ."

There are times when a number jumps out at him, and Francona will want to see the story in pictures. For example, he'll see one of his players with huge numbers against a pitcher, but further video investigation will show that those numbers were from 3 or 4 years ago. Or that a player who happens to be 2 for 12 against a pitcher actually has hit him hard, with no luck.

He doesn't feel the need to share his system with the players.

"No, I don't think the players have any idea how much time we spend with the preparation," he says. "That's fine. We want to—what's the word?—disseminate it so they can understand it easily and just play. We'll handle the information. They're good players; we just want them to go out and play."

So 7 months later, after thinking about the Yankees, spending like the Yankees, and wondering how they matched up with the Yankees, it was time for the Red Sox to do exactly what Francona said: go out and play—against the Yankees.

CHAPTER 7

Breakthrough

Hey, how's your dad?"

No matter where they were or what was at stake between their teams, their conversations always began the same way. Joe Torre would ask Terry Francona about his father, and the son would tell Tito that a former teammate was saying something nice about him. Torre and Francona would have their talks on the phone or sometimes in person, but usually out of fan and media view. They knew what the script was supposed to be, and if people knew how much genuine respect they had for each other—that they actually cared about the well-being of family members—hell, that just might ruin the whole movie.

They'd check in before a series began, before all the drama and storylines sucked them in, too. They'd keep it light, encourage each other with caveats—"Joe, I don't want you to win, but I wish you well"—and then get into their Yankees and Red Sox characters.

Torre would be sitting in the dugout with his blue Yankees cap pulled low, the brim straight-out-of-the-box stiff, and his arms folded over his chest. On warm days, when he wasn't wearing his jacket with "Yankees" scripted across the front, you could see the watch on his wrist; as epic as some of the Yankees–Red Sox games were, who could blame Joe for keeping track of his hours? Whenever he decided to take a trip to the mound, his steps often seemed robotic, like a machine that needs its hinges oiled.

"Joe, you look like shit," Francona once kidded him. "You walk the way I feel."

At Fenway, Francona could be found sitting near the dugout stairs. He'd have a huge wad of tobacco, neatly wrapped in bubble gum, stuffed in his jaw. He'd watch the game and also rock to it. He'd have on a red fleece jacket, which he wears now to stay warm, but in Philadelphia he wore it because it infuriated his critics. "It could be a thousand degrees and I'd have it on," he said. "I wore it because I knew it pissed people off. That's stupid, but that's how it all began; the more it aggravated people, the more I wore it."

Torre and Francona would take their positions and rarely glance in the other dugout. They both knew the history of the series: one Yankees–Red Sox game in 1978 capped a huge collapse for Torre's close friend Don Zimmer, who was Boston's manager; one game in 2003 had become the tipping point for Red Sox ownership and upper management to bring in Francona; four games the next year led to the greatest comeback—or collapse—in baseball history; and five games in 2006 had inspired the Red Sox to spend so much money that they wound up outbidding the Yankees—*outbidding the Yankees!*—by $18 million for the right to negotiate with Matsuzaka.

Neither manager ever came into these games unprepared. As friendly as they were, they were constantly looking for the edge that would make a difference in a close game or the inevitable close season series.

As they sat in their respective offices on the afternoon of April 20, 2007, they were planning to manage against one another for the 65th time since 2004. In the previous 64 games, including the playoffs, each of them had won 32 times. What 32 and 32 proved was that any sense of breathing room was an illusion. Okay, every once in a while, the matrix would have a glitch for four or five games. But the Yankees and Red Sox are the real-life versions of that classic B-movie scene: a struggle takes place, one fighter appears to be the lone survivor, and the seemingly pummeled body springs back to life for Round 2 . . . or Round 65.

That still didn't stop them from trying to create even the slightest separation. The new players weren't the only reasons the Red Sox were a little different in 2007. Francona had gotten management to agree to tweak the team's advance scouting system. In the past, a Red Sox advance scout would watch the Yankees play the Indians, and when it was time for the Red Sox to play one of those teams, the scout would be off to Toronto or Texas or wherever. Francona thought the advance scouts, Dana LeVangie and Todd Claus, did excellent work. He didn't understand why the scout who had studied Baltimore or New York would leave that city as the Red Sox were arriving there. Why not have them stay, be members of the coaching staff for a series, and take advantage of their insights in person?

His bosses agreed with him, and it was just one more thing that might be able to help him with his daily study sheets.

The other things that helped had nothing to do with the science of scouting. Once his work was done, he liked to make sure everyone was all right. Sometimes it meant answering a text from his daughter Alyssa, who needed his help on a crossword puzzle: "Hey Dad . . . lake in Nevada?" Often it was meeting up with rookie second baseman Dustin Pedroia for cribbage games in the manager's office. Like his father, Francona is known for treating clubhouse workers well, so there were times he'd playfully spar with worker Pookie Jackson. And before every game, he'd talk with Don Kalkstein, whom he trusted as much as anyone in the organization.

Kalkstein is a sports psychologist, burdened with the title of "director of performance enhancement." Francona met him in Texas in 2002, and was so impressed that he told Theo Epstein he had to hire him. "He's got a gift," Francona says. "He's a guy who's able to draw people to him, no matter where he is." It's a special gift because he is the embodiment of clubhouse confidential: whether you play or coach, you can tell him something and it stays with him. If he had been in Boston for Francona's first Yankees–Red Sox game, he could have calmed Francona before Francona calmed himself.

Of course, it always helps to have one of your best friends by your side as you go into an intense competition. After all these years, long after he made fun of those red Chuck Taylors in Tucson and told his friend to get ready for his first big-league at bat in Houston, Millsie was sitting next to Francona as his bench coach in Boston. It was 30 years later, and they were still boys. Millsie became family in Omaha, where Tito and Birdie practically adopted him and Ronda, his girlfriend who became his wife, at the 1979 College World Series.

There wasn't another manager–bench coach relationship like this in baseball.

Francona had held Millsie's first child, Taylor, the day she was born in 1981. Their families had spent holidays together and vacationed together. When Francona had sleepless nights as the Phillies manager, driving to Veterans Stadium at 3:30 in the morning, he'd call Millsie, who was one of his coaches: "Wake up. If I'm miserable, you have to be miserable, too." They were fired together after the 2000 season, and Francona went to work for the

Indians and Millsie went to the Cubs. They were scouting in Pittsburgh in September 2001, both staying at the Doubletree Hotel, when Francona got a call from Millsie: "Get up here, now. You have to see this." And they both stared in shock at the TV as they watched what was happening to New York City and the Twin Towers.

There wasn't anything they couldn't talk about, so sometimes baseball was easy compared to the real issues. They had the stamina to talk baseball all day, and sometimes they did.

While August 2006 was the worst time for the Red Sox to see the Yankees, April 2007 was the opposite. The pitching matchups were not in New York's favor. They were starting with a veteran, Andy Pettitte, and ending with two 24-year-old kids, Jeff Karstens and Chase Wright. The Red Sox were throwing their version of three aces at the Yankees: Curt Schilling, Josh Beckett, and the coveted Matsuzaka, who was known by his Americanized first name, Dice-K.

It was Yankees–Red Sox, and even 14 games into the season, it had the event feel of baseball's Opening Day and a Hollywood premiere's opening night. According to the stats, the leading hitter at the start of the series was J.D. Drew, who was hitting .375, but everyone's eyes saw a different story. Alex Rodriguez was hitting .371, which sounded low, because he seemed to be on everything. He already had 10 home runs, his swing looking more like June than April.

As the managers took their seats, immediately thinking three or four innings ahead of the crowd, the game began. Francona walked into the dugout with a secret card up his sleeve, holding onto a piece of information that wasn't known to a lot of people. He was already thinking about protecting that right shoulder of Jonathan Papelbon's, so since the closer had thrown 47 total pitches the previous two nights in Toronto, Francona had made a decision 5 hours before game time.

"He's not pitching tonight," he said in his office. "I don't care what the score is, he's not pitching tonight. It wouldn't be smart. He threw forty-seven pitches in two nights. He needs a night to regenerate."

Francona was so conscious of the shoulder that the night before, he called the bullpen and told coach Gary Tuck, "If we take the lead, Pap is pitching. But don't warm him up until we get the lead." Every pitch counts, even in warmups. If the Red Sox's half of the inning had ended too quickly and Papelbon didn't have enough time to get ready, Francona was prepared to go on the field and start an argument with umpires in order to buy a few more pitches.

Since Papelbon wasn't going to close in the first game of the Yankees series, Francona and pitching coach John Farrell huddled before the game and looked over Farrell's pitching charts.

"Do you know who's going to get a save tonight?" Francona said, wondering if Farrell had the same thought that he did.

"Hideki Okajima," Farrell responded.

"You got it," Francona said with a smile.

Okajima's first big-league pitch was blasted out of Kansas City's Kauffman Stadium, but since then his unusual style had been a marvel to opponents and teammates alike. The reliever would release the ball with his left hand and turn his head to the right, like a visionary point guard throwing a no-look pass. He didn't always see where his pitches landed, but neither did right-handed hitters, who found it difficult to get a good view of his curveball, which was superb, or his splitter.

The only issue with Okajima was that in his first year in the States, he wasn't used to the rhythms of a typical big-league reliever.

In spring training, he told Francona and Farrell that he needed two innings to get ready, which, in many cases, is about one and one-third innings more than he would normally have. They were able to work his two innings down to one by the time they broke camp.

All the talk of Red Sox saves seemed presumptuous with Rodriguez at the plate in the second inning. He was making a hard game look easy, even when pitchers got him out. When pitchers talk of making mistakes, they're usually talking about 2 or 3 inches. If Schilling happened to miss by that much, he knew that A-Rod was in such a groove that he could take a 3-inch mistake and send it 400 feet in any direction. Schilling got him to fly out to center in the second, but the hitter didn't appear to be fooled.

He came up again in the fourth, the Yankees leading 1 to 0, and he hit another fly ball. But this one was to left field and out of the park. What a pain. With the score tied at 2 in the fifth and two men on, the Red Sox and Schilling had a few things to worry about: the batting talent of Rodriguez and the sign-stealing ability of Rodriguez. Sometimes catcher Jason Varitek and Schilling would change their signs up to three times an at bat when facing Rodriguez. They didn't begrudge him for it; they did the same things.

"Everybody tries," Francona explained. "We try to steal third-base coaches' signs. They try to get ours. That's part of the game. You need to be good enough not to put down the first sign and let somebody know what's coming."

Even if Rodriguez knew exactly what Schilling was going to throw with his next pitch, what he did with it was scary. Schilling threw a fastball and missed by 2 inches, the width of a typical cell phone. Rodriguez, a right-hander, hit the ball like a left-handed pull hitter. Home run.

The wiseguy answer to Francona's pregame question—Do you know who's going to get a save tonight?—seemed to be New

York's distinguished closer, Mariano Rivera. The Yankees led 6 to 2 in the eighth, and that's when both managers began to give glimpses of their game theories.

Honestly, Torre surprised Francona in the bottom of the eighth. Scott Proctor had been on the mound, and he was taken out and replaced by Mike Myers. Francona didn't expect his buddy to bring out lefty specialist Myers to begin the eighth to face David Ortiz in a four-run game. He rocked and thought to himself, *This might be good, if not for today then for the next two games. Deception is how Myers gets guys out. Even if David doesn't get a hit here, we get a free look at Myers . . .*

The thoughts happen fast. The action is fast and intense: pitchers grunting with each ball thrown; the herdlike rumbling when a player is busting to beat a throw to first. Decisions must be made fast; if you feel that something is in your favor, you have to know how to take advantage of it quickly. It helps to have Ortiz on your side. His swing is as quick as a thought, so it didn't take long—two pitches—for Ortiz to see what he wanted from Myers and line it into center field for a double.

Old Fenway started to shake. Torre got up from his seat and took that mechanical walk to the mound. Myers was out, Luis Vizcaino was in. Francona looked at Millsie, just a look, and they both knew what it meant. *I think we've got something here.* Manny Ramirez walked, and the oldest and smallest park in baseball shook more, getting louder by the pitch. The fans in Boston mess with your mind, and they don't do it on purpose. They get a slight opening in an inning and they start thinking of the manager's ally, the crooked number, the big inning. They make you feel like you're losing when you're up 6 to 2 . . . or 6 to 3 after a Mike Lowell single.

It was time for Torre to walk again, and this time he was as serious as he had been all night. He was bringing out the King to put a stop to the nonsense. The ball was in the hands of Rivera. The Red Sox had to respect him and the greatness of his cut fastball, but they didn't fear him. They had faced him a lot, which meant that they had been trailing against the Yankees a lot. But because they had some familiarity with his stuff, they had a game plan against him. Varitek lined a run-scoring single, and the score was 6 to 4.

This is the reality of managing: You are married to your bullpen, specifically your closer. His good night is your good night. His bad night makes him wonder what he could have done differently, and it leads fans to suggest what *you* should have done differently.

It was just a ground ball. It was a ground ball pulled down the right-field line, and it happened to be hit by the fastest player in the park, Coco Crisp. Being at Fenway helped the center fielder, because when Crisp's ball hugged the line and rolled close enough to the fans to tempt them, they didn't reach over and touch it. Thus it was a ground ball that turned into a triple and a ground ball that tied the score at 6.

Which leads to one more note about being married to a closer: you can't take that measured walk to get him. You walk out there to take him out of the game, and you're no longer playing chess; you're playing 52 pickup. This was Rivera's game now. Who in that bullpen was capable of saving him? Alex Cora ended the suspense quickly for the Red Sox, lining a run-scoring single to left field to score Crisp with the go-ahead run.

Sometimes you can say what you want to do and it happens exactly the way you plan it. Sometimes you can sit on a couch in your office before the game, say that Hideki Okajima will get the save, and after a series of unpredictable events 8 hours later, he's in position to get it. It wasn't going to be easy for Okajima. He was going to have to go through Derek Jeter, Bobby Abreu, and A-Rod to get the save that had been predicted for him. Francona had a theory on Abreu: "I had Bobby for four years in Philadelphia. Bobby does not like facing a lefty for the first time. We've got to use that to our advantage. Because he doesn't want to be embarrassed, he'll take, take, take. You can sometimes get an easier out with an at bat like that. I've seen it happen numerous times."

The manager was one out of two on his predictions. Okajima handled Jeter and A-Rod easily. He made some good pitches to Abreu, who took and took until he saw ball four. One-run games are where second-guessers are bred, and so it was with the last batter of the game. The eighth had been a disaster for New York pitching, but Torre had made a move in the eighth that he would have liked to have had back in the ninth. Jason Giambi had singled in A-Rod to make the score 6 to 2, with no one out. The manager removed Giambi from first and replaced him with a pinch runner named Kevin Thompson.

The final out of the night was made by Thompson, a 27-year-old career minor leaguer. It was only April. It was just the 15th game of the season. It pushed Francona's career record against Torre to a modest 33 and 32. But the winning song of Fenway blared—"Dirty Water" by the Standells—and the city finally had a win over the Yankees to sleep on.

The next day, Francona sat in his office and talked baseball theory. It's a good manager's check of inventory, a quick assessment to see how he feels about the game. Francona loved to talk baseball and listen to other people talk about it as well. To hear someone discuss baseball is to learn a bit about how they process information and use it to make decisions. Francona enjoyed hearing and reading different philosophies, even when he disagreed with the analysis. He certainly had spent enough time around the

John Henry, Tom Werner, Larry Lucchino, and Theo Epstein—Theo and
The Trio—now have a manager who has twice delivered a prize that eluded
New England for 86 years. *(Cindy Loo/Boston Red Sox)*

Francona ended his playing career with the Milwaukee Brewers just as his father, Tito, did. He never fully recovered from a devastating knee injury. But he still managed to be a .274 hitter over ten seasons. *(AP Photos)*

With the Phillies, Francona and many of his players had a similar profile: young guy trying to make it. One of the veterans, Curt Schilling, was there for the losing in 1997, and for the winning—in Boston—in 2004 and 2007. *(AP Photos)*

Francona managed basketball legend Michael Jordan on the Birmingham Barons, the Chicago White Sox Double-A farm team. Their relationship gave him many insights on the psyche of stars and how to manage them.

(Birmingham News)

The scene that would change Red Sox baseball forever: Grady Little decided to leave Pedro Martinez on the mound in the eighth inning against the Yankees. Down by three, the Yankees would go on to tie the score and eventually win the game and the pennant, leading to Grady's departure and Francona's hiring. *(Brian Babineau/Boston Red Sox)*

Francona with Manny Ramirez, who, from a managerial perspective, is a player who requires explanation and elaboration. *(AP Photos)*

David "Big Papi" Ortiz knows how to handle a fastball and a clubhouse. Francona can mention any issue with the team and Ortiz will respond, "I'll handle it, bro." *(Julie Cordeiro/Boston Red Sox)*

The Red Sox got a boost in spring training when Jonathan Papelbon asked out of the rotation and reclaimed his closer's role. He restated his desire in July, when his employers consulted him—in an unusual meeting place—before acquiring Eric Gagne from Texas. *(AP Photos)*

Francona with Mike Lowell, who would become a key player in the 2007 season and would become the 2007 World Series MVP. *(Brian Babineau/Boston Red Sox)*

Dustin Pedroia was just 21 when he stared at his Red Sox bosses and said, "I can't begin to imagine why you guys would even think of sending me to [Single-A] Sarasota." Two years later, he won over his teammates with his bravado and skills. *(Brian Babineau/Boston Red Sox)*

Joe Torre used to watch Francona take candy from the Atlanta Braves' clubhouse in the 1960s when Francona's father, Tito, and Torre were teammates. In 2004, Torre and Francona began to play the roles of archenemies in baseball's most storied rivalry. *(Julie Cordeiro/Boston Red Sox)*

Epstein made Francona sweat while interviewing him for the job. Now they have the working relationship that Epstein dreamed of, one in which he can look at the manager and say, "I have the right to know why something happened—and vice versa." *(Brita Meng Outzen/ Boston Red Sox)*

Fittingly, Papelbon closed the Red Sox 2007 season with passion and panache. The kilt is from Boston rockers Dropkick Murphys, whose song "I'm Shipping Up to Boston" usually leads to a Papelbon dance. *(AP Photos)*

Francona holds the 2004 championship trophy during the victory parade, which New Englanders hadn't seen for four generations. (He's wearing the hat of his alma mater, the University of Arizona.) *(Cindy Loo/ Boston Red Sox)* game and seen enough great players to have some wise opinions—he and Tito played with a combined 22 Hall of Famers—but by no means was he a by-the-book type.

Talk of Crisp's triple down the right-field line the previous night naturally led to a discussion of guarding the lines in late innings.

"It might be called 'by the book'; I think it's covering your ass," he said. "I would rather put our team in the best position to win, and if someone hits a double I'll answer the question. You put two guys on the line, someone hits a single that shouldn't be a single, and when you lose nobody says anything. But that's not good . . . Dick Williams used to tell me, 'Stand directly on the line.' I would get so frustrated. Why am I standing here? You want me to catch some stuff in the stands?"

When Francona is busy, the clubhouse becomes more than a place where he can share his baseball beliefs. It can be a dentist's office, too. On the morning of the series' middle game, a game that contributed to Josh Beckett's season of redemption, the dentist came to Fenway and treated Francona in full uniform. He put temporary fillings in the manager's mouth, fillings that filled the grooves that Francona had from grinding his teeth. The filling work would be nothing compared to the drilling scheduled at the real dentist's office 2 days later.

Yankees–Red Sox may be difficult, but it's nothing like going to the dentist. It's baseball, and for the second consecutive day, it was winning baseball for the Red Sox. Ortiz hit another double—Mike Myers got him loose the night before—and hit a two-run homer. It was a good game, with the Red Sox winning 7 to 5, but no one wanted to talk about that as much as they did the debut of Dice-K against the Yankees on Sunday.

This series was what the fuss was all about, right? It's why Epstein actually wanted one of his employees to see the posting bid being submitted in New York, just in case someone tried to steal the pitcher away from him. Dice-K could pitch, but he had a lot to learn about the big leagues, and the Red Sox had a lot to learn about him. He was getting more comfortable, but Boras had been right about him. He was very formal whenever he went into Francona's office. When he struggled on the mound, he had to get used to Farrell or Francona coming out to talk with him. Francona soon learned that he wasn't used to that attention because he was usually counted on to get out of any jam in Japan. It was Dice-K, a Japanese legend; his manager there never felt the need to say anything to him while he was working.

There were many signs that he was adapting off the field. His intelligence allowed him to pick up formal English and slang quickly. He was a good listener, because he sometimes repeated the term of endearment that many of his teammates used as a greeting: "What's up, bitch?"

Showing just how short the American attention span can be, the pregame fascination with Dice-K was gone by the third inning. He wasn't the story anymore, and some of that had to do with his performance. He had given up two runs in the first inning, and three by the third. Fortunately, Dice-K was opposed by Wright, the young pitcher. He was coming off his big-league debut the start before, against the Indians. Sunday the 22nd was Francona's 48th birthday, but he wasn't concerned about gifts; he was more interested in finding what his team could get out of Wright.

"We had somebody watching him in Trenton and we've got video," Francona said of the rookie. "We know what he wants to do. If we make this guy throw strikes tonight, we should be okay."

Okay? Tell that to Jon Miller, the ESPN play-by-play man

who could barely keep his seat in the Fenway press box. The Red Sox trailed 3 to 0 until the third, when it seemed that they were beginning to chip away from the lead with a Ramirez home run. Then there was another home run by Drew. As Lowell stepped to the plate, no one in the park could have been thinking of back-to-back-to-back, could they? Even if it was just a young pitcher from the minors, it's hard for a team to be in sync like that. Isn't it? "And Lowell!" Miller said excitedly. "This one is headed to New Hampshire! This game is going to be tied up! What a shot! They're playing home run derby early this year at Fenway Park!" It was up to Jason Varitek to make it four in a row. The catcher is the definition of no-nonsense, from his crew-cut to the way he sprints around the bases after hitting a home run. He didn't have to wait long to sprint. Wright threw him a strike, and that ball, too, left the park, rocketing toward an appropriate sign with large block letters that read SPORTS AUTHORITY.

There were ten pitches and four home runs; it's safe to say that the Red Sox knew what Wright was trying to do. Speaking for themselves, they were just trying to sweep the Yankees. The man in the other dugout was managing with an urgency uncharacteristic of April. The most shocking example was seeing Torre go to Game 1 starter Pettitte in the third game, out of the bullpen. This was 52 pickup after all. Was the bullpen that thin where a veteran starter like Pettitte was forced into relief in April? If the Yankees were going to be playing well into October, they had better do something drastic with that bullpen.

The Red Sox walked away with yet another victory, 7 to 6, and although it wasn't a five-game sweep, it was all right. "We scored four more runs than they did, and we swept the series," Francona said. "Good for us. They'll be fine. We probably should have lost the first game and then we're fighting uphill. And instead we get to sweep. It's a funny game. You can't get too carried away with yourself."

It was Boston's turn to delight in the homecoming atmosphere and talk about getting some distance from New York. The Yankees would stumble and play some bad baseball, but they weren't going to go away. They rarely do.

CHAPTER 8

The Boiler Room

The expression on his face would have to do, because this wasn't the forum for his honest opinion. Dustin Pedroia was just 21 years old, the Red Sox's most recent top draft pick, so he would have to find a diplomatic way to take the edge off his thoughts. *Is this guy a clown? What game has he been watching?* After all, the man sitting across from him, Ben Cherington, was his boss.

It was 2005, and Pedroia was making his first spring training appearance since being drafted, 65th overall, in 2004. This was part of the drill. Cherington was in charge of player development, and one of his jobs was to meet individually with 150 minor league prospects and give them a plan for the year. Pedroia didn't need much. He had left Arizona State and immediately become an impact player in the low minors. He'd hit .336 in Sarasota and .400 in Augusta. Without anyone asking or telling him to do it, he had approached all of his teammates and told them that he liked to have as much fun as anyone, but he was in pro baseball to win.

He usually said whatever crossed his mind, but this time he toned down his language when Cherington said, "We haven't decided if you're going to go back to Sarasota [Single-A] or move on to Portland [AA]." Pedroia waited—*Idiots!*—and tried as hard as he could to play it down the middle: "I can't begin to imagine why you guys would even think of sending me to Sarasota." He looked around the room, stunned at the mere possibility of A ball, and kept that gaze until it was time for him to go. After Pedroia left, Cherington turned to coworkers Peter Woodfork and Rob Leary. "Well," the boss said. "I don't think we'll have to worry about staying on him."

Not unless they wanted to put their hands in an engine that was already running. Baseball evaluators talk a lot about pluses—a "plus" fastball, a "plus" arm—but Pedroia was a player of excess. It began with his self-confidence, which was so excessive that he had enough to heal the insecurities of all those in his social circle. The safe, buttoned-down crowd could look at him and see their opposite; Dustin Pedroia was the bold alter ego that they were too timid to embrace. He was a little man, 5 feet 8 inches on his tiptoes, with the exaggerated swing of a bopper. From afar, he looked like a bat boy doing a right-handed impersonation of Reggie Jackson.

Yes, the height. It always circled back to the height. His was the type of height that caused scouting department arguments. The Red Sox took him in the second round, and some of their scouts still believed that was a round or two too high. He was too short and too small to be a team's first selection. Jason McLeod, who was still a year away from becoming the Red Sox's scouting director, disagreed with them. McLeod kept coming back to the point—this kid is a definite big-leaguer—that should have been the greatest one of all. If you have a definite in a field known for being inexact, you go with the definite—even if it's a barely 5-foot-8-inch definite.

Whether it was Sarasota, Augusta, Portland, or Pawtucket, Pedroia wasn't going to be there long. His talent was going to take him to Boston, and his words would ensure that he wouldn't be forgotten once he arrived.

In 2007, Pedroia got hot at the same time the Red Sox did. The April expectations were low for the rookie second baseman, and he still didn't meet them. He hit .182 for the month and, for a while, split time with veteran infielder Alex Cora. But as the season moved toward the back end of May, both Boston's divisional lead and Pedroia's batting average began to grow. What the Red Sox were doing to the American League East bordered on embarrassing. Going into a game against the Rangers on a pleasant Sunday afternoon in Texas, Boston had an 11-game advantage over second-place . . . Toronto. The Yankees were in third place, 12½ games behind. As for Pedroia, May would be about, naturally, excess. He was on his way to hitting .415 for the month, and for the game against the Rangers on the 27th, his season average was .271.

Pedroia had already proven that he could manage the most difficult of dances: showing enough modesty to satisfy the veterans, but also entertaining them with his material, which only landed on modesty by accident. They teased him, mostly about his height, but they liked him and his stuff. Even on the days when Cora played over him, the veteran would make a point to pull Pedroia aside. "I'm playing today, but this job is yours."

The rookie started the game against the Rangers on the 27th, and when he stepped in the box in the ninth inning, he was looking to get his second hit of the day. It was going to be tough, because he was facing a closer, Eric Gagne, who hadn't given up a run all season. It was popular to say that Gagne wasn't what he used to be, which was true, but the whole story was that he was the king of National League closers for 3 years running. He had one Cy Young Award sandwiched between two Top 10 finishes. He was a Stan Lee comic book character come to life: oversized goggles, body of an NFL blocking back, and possessor of a fastball-changeup combination that allowed him to convert a major league record 84 consecutive saves. No, he was not what he used to be, but he was still very good.

The Rangers were trailing 5 to 4, and Gagne's job was to wipe out the number-nine hitter, Pedroia, and the top of the order. The easiest pitch he threw to Pedroia was the first one, a strike. Then it was time for a one-on-one version of Texas Hold 'Em, with Gagne throwing every pitch he had, and Pedroia fouling them all off. Pitch 5 fouled off, Pitch 6, Pitch 7, Pitch 8, all fouled off. Once Gagne backed off the mound and shrugged at the Red Sox dugout. *Where in hell did you get this little dude?* Pitch 9, fouled off. Pitch 10, my God, fouled off—and fouled off with that oversized swing. On Pitch 11, someone would have to crack. This was the showdown, right? This was baseball. Damn. This stubborn little . . . He fouled it off again.

Finally, on Pitch 12, with the count forever frozen at 2–2, it was time to see who had the best hand. Forget about being cute. It was Eric Gagne versus a number-nine hitter named Pedroia. Let the best man win with his go-to goods: Gagne threw a fastball right down the middle, and Pedroia swung for the fences, a swing offensive to those who have automatic quotes prepared for the 5-8-and-under set: "Son, you have to choke up on the bat . . ." Uh-uh. No choke-ups. This was Pedroia's pitch, and he got enough of it to send it over the left-field wall for a home run.

He rounded the bases, and that was the exciting part for the Red Sox in the dugout; they knew he would come back with something outrageous to say, and he didn't disappoint. As he gave out high-fives and received taps on the head, he told his teammates, "That motherfucker had better develop another pitch!"

They rolled.

He was the best kind of comedian in that it was always funnier coming from him; extra-large bravado from a bigger man who looked the part would have been expected, but Pedroia made it ironic. And like those great comics, you got the sense that some of the best lines were borne from slights that produced frustration before laughter.

None of that mattered in June, because Pedroia had a manager who was a fan of his. For Terry Francona and anyone else leading a team, the highest compliment you can pay a player is saying that you trust him: trust him to prepare to win; trust him to have the ability to do the job; and trust him to make the necessary corrections to issues that might arise. Francona trusted Pedroia, so much so that by early June, his days at the bottom of the lineup were over.

Pedroia had hated the first month of the season, when he felt held back by the combination of his average and one fewer at bat per game, which prevented him from getting into a rhythm. His opportunity came, and it came because half of the news was good: he was crushing the baseball. On June 15, after a five-hit game against the Giants, his average sparkled at .331 and his on-base percentage was .406. In that game, he caught up to one of Barry Zito's curveballs and hit his first home run since the showdown in Texas.

"All right, fellas," he said as he entered the dugout. "I'm taking cash, checks, and credit cards."

He *was* a money player. He didn't walk a lot, but he didn't strike out a lot, either. He could hit, which meant a lot of doubles would come off that bat of his at Fenway Park. He was able to play at a high level, take verbal abuse from his teammates, and still maintain his own personality. Francona would search for him daily, making sure that he wasn't avoiding those cribbage games. They'd sit and talk about everything, things that happened on the field included.

"Why are you running for me in games?" Pedroia asked.

"Because you're slow," Francona answered.

Pedroia would shake his head—he didn't think he was *that* slow—and the manager would smile. He always knew that Pedroia was fuming when he ran for him, as he had at the end of June in another game against Texas. That time, at Fenway, Pedroia had gotten an eighth-inning double off Gagne's setup man, Akinori Otsuka. The Red Sox were trailing 5 to 4 with two outs, and Kevin Youkilis was at the plate. Francona motioned for Julio Lugo to run for Pedroia. *What game has he been watching?* Lugo came in, tried to steal third, and was caught stealing. On that night, Gagne was spared from facing Pedroia in the ninth. He got his save the "easy" way, striking out David Ortiz and getting Manny Ramirez to ground out.

On the morning after the loss, July 1, the Red Sox were 10½ games ahead of the Yankees. And everybody in New England knew it. For the handful of people who went to bed without Red Sox information, the top three morning questions were: "How did the Sox do last night? . . . Okay, what about the Yankees? . . . So, I know the traffic on 128 is ridiculous; how bad is it?"

It was at least a misdemeanor in Boston to suggest that the East race was over, and that the New Yorkers were too old and slow to make it competitive. Too many people remembered the Collapse of '78, and they talked about it the same way old-timers discussed Black Tuesday and the stock market crash of '29. If they didn't remember '78, they'd had it recited to them many times over family dinners and at family reunions. It was part of that running dialogue that Theo Epstein knew so well. It truly was Leslie Epstein and family's introduction to Boston: the Rhodes Scholar novelist and professor took a teaching position at Boston University—he had lived in New York—and settled in Brookline in 1978.

History aside, the Yankees were playing a lot better. It was foolish to dismiss a team with their talent and ability to acquire more of it. With that said, the Yankees were still a week away from having more wins than losses, and they hadn't been in that position since being swept by the Red Sox in April.

But remember, just half of the news was good. There had been a reason Pedroia was able to slide into a top-of-the-lineup opening. Two of the players that the Red Sox paid with cash, checks, and credit cards, Lugo and J.D. Drew, were not performing as well as expected.

Lugo's slump had begun the season before in Los Angeles, where he had been traded from Tampa Bay. He didn't produce in the second half of 2006, and the drought followed him into 2007. He was a good player, but his average on July 1 was .190 and there were some minor adjustment issues that needed to be worked out. As is his style, Francona talked with Lugo at a moment when the shortstop was in the best environment to receive the information. One day during batting practice, he draped his arm around Lugo's shoulder, and it was like two old buddies talking. It was actually brilliant; the conversation was about Lugo doing everything he could to learn the team's signs. It was a casual setting with a very specific message. The manager's arm was draped there, a few inches from being a headlock, and it wasn't moving until the message had been delivered.

Drew was not a player in need of a talking-to. He knew where he was supposed to be and he was usually there, not an hour early, mind you, but never late, either. He came from a family that should be considered one of Georgia's natural baseball resources: three baseball-playing Drew boys, all of them first-round picks, and all of them able to say that they made it to the big leagues. J.D. was jazz-DJ smooth in everything he did on the field. He had an easy swing at the plate, a swing that had infinitely more power than it appeared to have. He was fast, running with just-right strides and no wasted motion. He had the skills to play center field if you asked or he could shift over to right at Fenway, which was the largest and trickiest right field in baseball.

So what was the problem? Nothing. Actually, it was nothing that you could touch and say, "Aha!" He had smoked that ball against the Yankees in April, the four-homer game, but on July 1, that home run represented the last one Drew had struck against an American League team. That span of soft lineouts, walks, and strikeouts, and no homers, had reached 52 games. He had been brought in to provide protection for Ortiz and Ramirez, and he was protecting them; he was protecting them from seeing good pitches. He wasn't hurt. He didn't limp. He didn't throw his bat. He went up, he walked or struck out, and he sat down.

That was the part of Drew that Bob Ryan was sighing over, with most of the region sighing along with him. It had been a long time since Boston was the Boston of the high-mannered Brahmins. This was no polite society that sat on strong opinions until the "appropriate" time. Any time at the ballpark was the appropriate time. Drew wasn't producing and he wasn't emoting the way passionate Boston fans wanted. They occasionally let him know about it, but even the way he absorbed criticism was smooth. He'd strike out, tuck his bat under his arm, and coolly put it into the bat rack.

Francona had to juggle the lineup, and he let Lugo and Drew know before he did it. It was perceived as a touchy-feely approach, especially by the old-school managers, but Francona saw it differently and more simply. He believed that both of them were good players who would eventually get hot. But, more important, like most managers, he was looking ahead. Several innings ahead—like to September and October. The Collapse of '78 wasn't part of his childhood or adult life—his "running dialogue" was the 1970s Pittsburgh Steelers—so he was confident that his team was going to win the division and be in the playoffs.

"We may not run away with it the way people want us to," he said. "But we should be okay." *Okay* was a Francona euphemism; *okay* meant "I'll be shocked if this doesn't happen."

Since he was looking ahead, he first thought of maintaining the morale of both players. He knew they'd eventually hit, but he didn't want their new lineup roles to put a drag on their spirits. He talked to both players and found that they were both fine with baseball. Like anyone else who is charged with managing people, Francona's most challenging work would be monitoring what happened away from the field.

Overall, by Boston standards, the season was quiet. There was usually some moment—on the radio, in print, on a blog, somewhere—when the long-running local series, "Manny Being Manny," got some attention. It could be the controversy of a Manny off day. It could be Manny not showing up at the All-Star Game. Or it could be some play in the field that is an affront to a baseball fan, a fan who never saw (insert name of 1960s player) do things like that and never saw (insert name of 1960s manager) stand for it. There were no Manny Moments in July. A week before the trading deadline, there were three major stories in town.

One was about basketball, and it got Francona's attention. The word was that the Celtics were close to making a major trade that would bring forward Kevin Garnett to town. Francona already liked watching the Celtics, mostly because his friend Doc Rivers was the head coach. But he would obsess over the team if they were able to have a lineup featuring Garnett, Ray Allen, and Paul Pierce.

The other two stories were related to the team that Francona managed. They were also trade rumors. Francona may have been patient with Drew, but most of the fans had seen enough. There had been talk of Jermaine Dye, struggling with the White Sox, being traded to the Red Sox. Francona was in Oakland when Dye played there, and he was confident that there would be no issues, playing time included. He considered Dye one of the best and most professional players in baseball, so he wasn't worried about any type of sulking as he figured out a way to rotate a new outfielder among the team's starters and young reserve Wily Mo Pena.

There were also rumblings that Texas was going to make its comic book closer, Gagne, available. Gagne had an ERA of 2.16, almost identical to Jonathan Papelbon's 2.15. Gagne had blown one save all season and given up the homer to Pedroia; Papelbon had blown two saves and given up four home runs. The Rangers were looking for prospects, and not necessarily prospects that would be considered to be in an organization's top five or top ten. It sounded interesting and doable. There was just one question: what would the Red Sox do with Gagne?

The proof was there for all to see. He was a closer, Papelbon was a closer, their numbers were similar, end of conversation. Gagne had never been a setup man in his career, so there was no reason to think that he would want to do that job in Boston. To make a deal even more unlikely, the Red Sox had Hideki Okajima setting up, and he was no longer a surprise to the league. He was an All-Star, and his ERA was 0.87. If Gagne were to come to Boston and set up, he'd lose out on the incentives—save incentives—that were likely to trigger his bonus. And he also had a no-trade clause.

You name it, and it was there; all the baseball reporters could call their editors on the day of the trading deadline—July 31 at 4:00 P.M. EDT—and report that a mountain of evidence suggested that this trade was bogus. Or they could have done, unbelievably, what the Red Sox were planning to do: they could have called Papelbon and asked what his thoughts were on the potential deal.

Epstein and everyone else in baseball operations had been working the phones all day, trying to see if they could pull off the deal with Chicago for Dye—it was fading—or the one with GM Jon Daniels in Texas for Gagne—it was warming up. Gagne was represented by Scott Boras, who rivaled commissioner Bud Selig and players association head Donald Fehr for the following title: most powerful man in baseball without a team affiliation. Boras reported that his client was open to coming to Boston if he could close.

At 1:00, in one of the strangest sights of the season, four men stuffed themselves in a car and went on a one-mile road trip: Francona, Epstein, pitching coach John Farrell, and bullpen coach Gary Tuck. Francona was in full uniform. They left Yawkey Way and, after a couple of quick turns, were in Papelbon's neighborhood. It may have been the first time that the quartet had been on the clock and on a meter at the same time.

About that meter: they were on Boylston Street in Boston, a few doors from where Francona had one of his first meals during his Boston interview. It was a busy Tuesday at midday, and finding an open meter at that hour in the city probably means that you're being set up to be on the TV show *Punk'd*. They decided to park illegally near a steak house, Abe & Louie's, and Francona shouted to someone inside, "Just don't let them tow it, all right?"

It was 3 hours before the deadline, and they needed to know if their idea could be put in motion. They had no problem with Pap. They loved the guy. They thought they could shorten games the rest of the season by throwing out Okajima, Papelbon, and Gagne in succession. They were right about the theory. But the reason they were standing on Boylston Street, with the manager in uniform, was that they knew the psychology of a true closer.

It's hard to find a man who doesn't mind having all the pressure on him at the end of games. The pitchers who like it love it, and they love it so much that it becomes an addiction. It's one of the reasons Papelbon was dragging a bit in spring training. Epstein saw him as a starter; he saw himself as a closer. He liked hearing "Wild Thing" playing for him as he knocked fists with a police officer, Billy Dunn, and raced out of the bullpen door. He liked that he could just deal in short bursts: splitter, fastball, sometimes slider. He'd pound his glove at the end of it, point his finger at Jason Varitek or Doug Mirabelli, and then listen to "Dirty Water" as his teammates celebrated another win on the field. Dynamic duos for one job usually means one of two things: you don't have one good thing (i.e., two mediocre quarterbacks in football) or you've got one out-of-sorts performer, used to the spotlight, now forced to sing backup.

At least they were trying. They wanted to speak with Papelbon in his condo, but there was no place to sit in private. He had several people in his place, helping him organize memorabilia for a signing, and there was stuff strewn all around. What they could do is go to a room downstairs and speak in peace. It was the building's boiler room. It wasn't that big, and not all of them would have the luxury of sitting in a chair, but they wouldn't be bothered. And they wouldn't have to strain to hear one another because the space was so tight. The five men went into the room, the key to the building, and talked to the most important member of their bullpen about the possibility of setting up games for Gagne. It was awkward. It was already hot in Boston from the recent heat wave.

And now they were a little hotter in a hot room. Furthermore, they were broaching a topic that Papelbon listened to, but it was a topic with which he wasn't comfortable.

He didn't know what they were coming over to talk about. Francona had called and said they'd be there shortly. "Don't worry," the manager had said on the phone. "You're not in trouble and you're not getting traded." Improving the team made sense to all of them, and Papelbon could understand their point once they explained it. But this was one of those situations of organizational intelligence that Francona dreamed of in Oakland: The Ivy Leaguers had an idea, the player had a different idea, and the sides agreed to meet in the middle. Papelbon did appreciate the respect of a face-to-face visit, and he would tell Francona that later during a long chat.

But he wanted to close. He just wasn't excited about anything else.

All around, it was suddenly becoming less comfortable. Two days after Pedroia's homer off Gagne, May 29, the Red Sox were 36–15, 14½ games ahead of the Yankees. Since then, the Red Sox were 28–27 and the Yankees were 36–20. The optimistic view was that the Red Sox had given themselves enough of a cushion to be average; the optimists were starting to get competition. The lead over the Yankees was down to seven games.

Fortunately for the traveling Red Sox, the car was still there after they talked in the stifling boiler room. They still had time to work something out with Boras. He was informed that Papelbon wasn't on board with giving up his job, so would Gagne be interested in another role? They'd even pick up his bonus.

As the deadline approached, they were clear on this much: Papelbon was still their closer, Okajima would still be used as a setup man, just bumped up an inning, and Gagne had agreed to come to

Boston for the rest of the season—with the knowledge that he would not be the closer. On that day, the 31st, they had also gone to reserve Eric Hinske and asked if he wanted to be traded. They liked him a lot, and wanted to be sure he was happy, even if they couldn't promise him playing time. Hinske appreciated the thought, but he enjoyed being a part of a winning group. Francona was appreciative, knowing, as he said about himself, "I didn't wake up in the morning excited to be the left-handed pinch hitter." Players who didn't get as much time and were still pros about it impressed the manager.

As for Gagne, it didn't take long for the acquisition to backfire.

He said all the right things, tried to be a great teammate, said he was happy to be close to his native Montreal, pitching for the Red Sox. He had a good attitude. His location was terrible. The fans turned on him for good during an August weekend in Baltimore. On a Friday night, he took the ball in the eighth inning with the Red Sox winning 5 to 1. He left without closing the inning, and the Red Sox lost that game. Two days later, in the series finale, he had a chance to redeem himself. He entered the game in the eighth inning in relief of Mike Timlin. There was a runner on base and Miguel Tejada was at the plate.

"There's a long drive to left field . . ."

He gave up a home run, and the Red Sox lost in extra innings.

A lead that had been 14½ was now down to 4. Four! Boston's baseball landscape was no longer quiet; the city was angry, and there were plenty of people identified as targets. Epstein was on the list because he traded for Gagne. Francona was on the list because he called his number. And Gagne was on the list because he was the jinx perceived as single-handedly ruining the season. *Gagme* became the street name for the man wearing number 83.

One day, when the team was back at Fenway, Francona sat next to Gagne and started a conversation.

"Hey," the manager said, "I'm no expert on pitching. But I'm here for you. If you go down, big boy, I'm going down with you."

Gagne exhaled and went to work—hard—and it never got better for him. He was so determined to turn things around that he studied each pitch that he had thrown the entire season. That number on August 19, when he actually had a decent performance against the Angels, was 700. He sat there like a coach, trying to see a trend in some sequence of those 700 pitches. Was it his arm slot? Where he was standing on the rubber? Was it velocity? Was he tipping pitches?

Or was it in his head?

It was getting tight for all of them. There were more references to 1978. There were polls asking if winning the division was as important as getting into the playoffs. There were more talk-radio callers wondering if Francona was too loyal to his players.

The Red Sox were able to pad the cushion and get it back to 7½ going into a series at Yankee Stadium. But all was not well. Manny had a strained oblique muscle, and the timetable on that was impossible to project. While Pedroia was still hitting—the kid was holding steady at .319—Drew and Lugo still hadn't cracked .265. Gagne had a sore shoulder. Ortiz had a knee that was going to need surgery at the end of the season. And while there had been discussions about a contract extension for Francona earlier in the year, it had not been talked about in months.

The Red Sox had an off night in New York City on Monday, August 27, and Francona didn't stay in his room to watch the Yankees–Tigers game on ESPN. He missed a 16 to 0 Tigers victory, viewed with interest in Detroit, New York, and Boston. He stood by his controversial stance that he had to worry about his team, not the Yankees, so he just couldn't spend all his energy following them pitch by pitch.

Instead, he left his room at the Westin Times Square and traveled about eight blocks with the entire family. His son, Nick, came up from Washington, where he was an intern at a think tank (he had studied Japanese in high school). The girls were there: Alyssa, who was at the University of North Carolina; Leah, who would be there soon; Jamie, the youngest, an athlete and writer; and Jacque, a nurse and his wife of 26 years. They all went to Uncle Jack's Steakhouse in Manhattan. Francona had the surf and turf and a couple glasses of white wine; they did not talk baseball.

Even if the Yankees had won that game with Detroit it would have been all right with him. He wanted to crush the Yankees in the division just like Joe Torre and the Yankees wanted to crush him. He knew how big the games in New York were, and he'd be lying if he said the Yankees hadn't cost him sleep. But the games, the criticism, the pressure, and the disappointment were nothing compared to what he'd been through in the past.

CHAPTER 9

Life After Death

Birdie Francona told her only son that it would be all right, that there was no reason to worry or fuss. They both knew that this day might have been random on other calendars, but it deserved a special notation on each of theirs. Earlier in the spring of 1988, Birdie had discovered a lump on one of her breasts. She had it checked out, and now, a few weeks later, this was the day the doctor would give her the news.

She was in New Brighton, Pennsylvania, and Terry was in Portland, Oregon. Only she could make a phone call from thousands of miles away seem like a conversation from front porch to front porch; only she could be calm and comforting when repeating the doctor's news: she had breast cancer. It didn't matter that Tito told a different story when he picked up the phone. "Your mother has some serious things going on here," he said. Birdie was convincing, and if she said it was going to be all right and that he should enjoy playing baseball, he believed it.

Birdie had always found a way to adapt to the unexpected. Why would this be any different? Her first surprise as a Francona came in the early 1960s, when she and Tito moved from her hometown—Aberdeen, South Dakota—to New Brighton. What a culture shock. She hadn't met any Italian Americans before she fell in love with Tito—she hadn't met any African Americans, either—and suddenly she had a father-in-law who spoke in several tongues: Italian, English, and whatever the Spirit moved him to say when he was preaching at the Italian Christian Center. She hadn't seen anything like that church, the piano-playing and piano-tuning man who led it, or the people who lived around Honky Alley, the ethnic neighborhood that surrounded it.

Everything was just a little different about this place, about 40 miles northwest of Pittsburgh. It was a small-town melting pot and Birdie became the salt of it. Everyone loved Birdie and Tito, and not just because Tito played pro ball for Cleveland, the closest American League team in the region. They were real people who attended their churches, sent their kids to their schools, shopped at their stores (Birdie loved the meat at Pullion's Market), and worked blue-collar jobs just like them. Tito worked part-time for the county's recreation department to supplement the income he made from baseball. He also was a basketball official, and a damn good one, who was first assigned all the big high school games. He started to work his way up to Duquesne and Pitt games, but then Birdie told him to stop; it was too time-consuming.

Or maybe the protective mother and wife—the mother who was willing to fight all of Phillips 66 to protect the rights of her boy—was leery of her husband's controversial calls. One night, officiating a game between Chester and Aliquippa, Tito made sure he got an emotional game under control by giving a technical to a player from Aliquippa. Terry, a basketball fan and preteen, watched the whole play and talked to his father afterward.

"Dad, you gave the one kid a technical, and it was the kid on the *other* team who hit him first."

Tito listened to his son, paused, and said, "You're right. I kind of thought that's what happened."

They looked at each other, father and son, and cracked up laughing. All of the Franconas—Tito, Birdie, Terry, and his younger sister Amy—shared a lot of laughs in that small town, tucked into the splendid Allegheny Mountains.

There was a reason Terry called his mother a saint. She was sweet, even when she was trying to get his attention. When she got mad at him, she'd still cook him dinner, but she'd make beef stew, his least favorite meal. That was a serious punishment because he looked forward to all of Birdie's meals. Most of the time he couldn't imagine anyone making better food than his mother. (Jacque now has all of Birdie's recipes.) There was the time, though, when she got a little too experimental on him. He was eating one of her creations and said, "Mom, what's this?" Her answer nearly ruined his appetite for a week: "Tongue." He politely asked Birdie to please, please never cook tongue again.

They shared laughs everywhere, really. Tito insisted on taking his baseball pension at 45 years old—"You never know what life will bring"—and he and Birdie used some of that money to travel to Omaha. They watched Terry play in the College World Series, fell in love with Millsie and his girlfriend Ronda, and smiled a lot, even when Terry's team didn't win the whole thing.

And today, like yesterday, was going to be all right. That's what Birdie wanted Terry to believe as he prepared to play as an outfielder for the Colorado Springs Sky Sox. They were in Portland to play the Beavers in a Pacific Coast League game; that part was understandable. The puzzling part was why he was there to begin with.

He had invited himself to spring training with the Indians in 1988. He had gotten himself into good shape, the best he had felt in 3 years. He dominated with the minor leaguers, where the Indians had put him, so they let him play with the big boys. He kept getting hits there, too. Doc Edwards, the Indians manager and one of Tito's old Cleveland teammates, called Francona into the office.

"You're going to have a great year," Doc told him. "You're going to be my number-two hitter."

A few days later, president and general manager Hank Peters had a different idea. The story in all the country's major newspapers began this way: "The Cleveland Indians, unwilling to start the season with the recently acquired Terry Francona as their first baseman, bought the contract of Willie Upshaw yesterday from the Toronto Blue Jays . . ."

It was time for another meeting with Doc.

"Terry, you've been around this game for a long time," Doc said. Francona nodded. He knew this speech. He was all ready for Doc to tell him that he was going to be Upshaw's backup. "We're going to send you down," the manager announced.

So he wound up in Colorado Springs, where there was a carnival and a baseball game taking place daily, both at the same time. There was one game in May when the Sky Sox gave up 12 runs and still beat the Phoenix Firebirds by 21 runs. Yes, the final score was 33 to 12. There was another time when manager Steve Swisher got so mad at Francona that he threw an entire container of beer on him. Still, Francona enjoyed playing for and talking with Swisher. He enjoyed playing there in the thin air, one call away from the majors.

That's Americana, isn't it? You're always one phone call away from being discovered. Or you're always one phone call away from hearing news so bad that it makes you think more of exceptions and hyperbole than the drudgery of the news itself: *Maybe they made a mistake; doctors can make mistakes, too; and if it is true, she's going to beat that disease like it stole something . . . cancer is not ready for my mother . . .*

In July, it sure seemed like Birdie was right about being all right. After playing in the same area in which he had been a minor leaguer seven years earlier, Francona was deemed to have paid his dues. The Indians called him up, allowing him to play for the same team that Tito had for six seasons. He was close to New Brighton now, so if Birdie needed him for anything, it was easier to see her from fewer than 150 miles away.

This city, this stadium, and this team were mocked nationally, but it felt like home to Francona. All the mosquitoes, empty seats, losses, and incessant drum-banging, which were part of the Indians experience, didn't discourage him. He knew old Italians in the city who looked out for his father. He knew policemen and security guards and clubbies, who all knew Tito. The first time Francona got a hit at creaky Cleveland Municipal Stadium, a man named Cy Buynak began to cry; he had joined the Indians in 1961 and remembered looking after a young Francona when Tito was busy playing.

Back in New Brighton, Birdie looked strong. She appeared to be healthy, bright, and alert as he finished the season in Cleveland with a .311 average. Not only was she there for that season, she survived the rest of his career, too.

He didn't plan it this way, but he was now retracing some of his father's steps. The last stop of Tito's big-league career was Milwaukee, in 1970, and it was the last stop of his son's, in 1990. His playing days ended with an unforgettable and nonspecific memento: an ache. It was an ache all over his body, an ache from years of playing when he wasn't supposed to, an ache from constantly trying to show that he was physically gifted enough to play when he truly wasn't. His career ended because he wasn't good enough. As soon as he was released in spring training with St. Louis—Tito had played there, too—he put all his equipment away, never to be tempted by thoughts of a comeback, and instead focused on his real life.

It became a real life fast, almost at the hour of his release in 1991. His parents needed his help in New Brighton. Birdie had chased off cancer the first time, in 1988, and she had been doing well. But cancer is a cruel disease, randomly searching for another place to establish itself in the body, and dammit, it came back. And it came back strong. Birdie's son had no idea how sick she had been and how hard she had been fighting, fighting even as she told him not to worry. She had been able to smile while her body was at war, but the cancer was relentless, and it began to attack her cells and her spirit. She was moving slowly from chemotherapy, and now her primary caretaker, Tito, needed someone to take care of him.

Tito was coming off open-heart surgery, so he needed assistance for his wife and himself. Since there were no more games for Francona to play, he and Jacque were able to go to Pittsburgh, get an apartment there for a few weeks, and help out in New Brighton. They were able to stay long enough to see Tito get stronger, and to see Birdie, still not showing just how sick she was, pushing back as the cancer moved forward. It was one woman against an army, and she was able to delay what was slowly becoming inevitable for over a year.

In the fall of 1992, Francona was finishing up his first season as a manager in the White Sox system, with Single-A South Bend. He got a call from Tito, who told him that he should get to New Brighton the next day to see his mother. Francona had a phone conversation that night with Birdie.

"Mom, I'll be home tomorrow," he said.

"Okay."

When he got to New Brighton, she didn't recognize him. Even

sadder, he didn't recognize her. The cancer had spread to her brain, to her face, all over her body. Whatever energy she had left was devoted to taking away that pain, that persistent pain. Her son would go into her room and check on her, and 5 minutes later, she wouldn't remember that he had been there. Tito had taken care of her as best as he could, he and all of New Brighton. They sat with him, brought him food, did anything they could to help out Birdie. But strong drugs needed to be stronger, large doses needed to be larger, just for her to have a bit of comfort.

In the hospital, Tito finally told his son to go home. And not the home of Pullion's, the New Brighton Hot Dog Shop, and the fields where he could always hear Tito's whistle. He told him to go back to Tucson, because he didn't need to see his mother like this. She was in so much pain that she was trying to do the impossible and escape her body. They strapped her to her bed to keep her calm and give her more medication.

So Francona left, knowing that he was coming back soon. He got in his car and drove from Beaver County, Pennsylvania, to Tucson, Arizona. He was always compared to his father, for obvious reasons, and that didn't bother him; he played the same sport as his father, he looked like his father, he had the same nickname as his father, and he loved his father deeply. But now he would have to be more like his mother. He was going to have to adapt to a new reality, just as she did when she left Aberdeen for New Brighton. Her life changed and she had to figure out what that new life, in an unfamiliar place, was going to be. His life was changing, too. Birdie knew him as a baseball player, and he knew her as the saintly mother who always made everything better. These two realities were splitting, with the baseball player retiring and the mother taking her place among the saints.

Birdie died in September 1992. Just as he knew he would when he left the hospital a week earlier, Francona boarded a plane and returned to New Brighton for the service. He saw her there in that casket and . . . you just have to know what it's like to be around someone you love, that person being slowly taken away by a disease and tortured by that disease. The goal is always healing, but sometimes healing means serenity and no pain. He saw her there in that casket and he cried and smiled, too, because she finally looked like Mom again: she was beautiful and at peace.

The service was almost 10 years to the day that Birdie's father-in-law, Carmen Francona, died after listening to a baseball game. His grandson had arrived at that service on crutches after suffering his first major injury as a professional. That day, as much as he knew Tito would miss his father, Francona knew that Tito still had Birdie; they had each other, and they'd always take care of one another. But in September 1992, who did Tito have to take care of him? His son was worried about him. He'd invite his father out to Arizona to get away for a while and relieve his mind, temporarily, from loss and loneliness. They tried doing something that both of them loved, golf, and they would play on some wonderful courses in Arizona. They would begin to play the game they loved and, unexpectedly, Tito would break down and cry. His son wasn't the only one who knew how special his wife was.

After a few years, Tito figured out a way to forever honor his wife and her memory. He put together a charity golf tournament along with a dinner and dance, with the proceeds going to the hospital that helped him so much with Birdie. With each passing year, he was able to celebrate the entirety of her life, and not just recall the 4 years when they learned medical terms that they would have rather left to the medical journals.

One thing that father and son needed to pay particular attention to was the heart; the Francona men had a history of heart disease and heart attacks. It wasn't just Carmen and Tito. There were numerous cousins and uncles and brothers who didn't make it, and they didn't make it because of some trouble with their hearts. What made these men scary was how tough they all were; they had incredible pain thresholds, so family and friends needed to stay on them to go to the hospital. The Francona men would dismiss some things, things that would leave some men doubled over in pain, for hours at a time. Francona didn't know if his father was joking 7 years ago after a round of golf, but the fact that he wasn't sure how serious Tito was speaks to the strength of the man.

"I had a heart attack on the seventh hole," Tito told his son. "And I had a horrible back nine."

A joke? Francona knew his father was tough enough and strong enough to play through any mild heart attack and then do something about it later. What wasn't a joke was the night, shortly after the golf story, when Tito became one of those Francona men who didn't make it. And then he made it again. It was a night of dancing and celebration in memory of Birdie, and Tito was thanking all of the doctors and nurses who had helped his wife. All he remembers was dancing and then blacking out. His eyes rolled back into his head and he collapsed. He was dead. He doesn't remember anything about a commotion, a crowd gathering around him, and someone rushing a doctor to a car to get a defibrillator. He doesn't remember being shocked once, and then twice, before coming to and taken to the hospital.

Someone had called his son, who was living in Philadelphia at the time. It was 11:00 in the evening when Francona got the call about his father. He didn't have time to wait for a flight, because the first one from Philadelphia to Pittsburgh wasn't going to leave until early the next morning. He needed to get there as quickly as he could. He put some things in a bag, got in his car, and drove the

5½ hours from eastern Pennsylvania to the western part of the state.

He arrived at the break of dawn, early enough to see his father awake and then not awake; it was happening again. Now, a doctor had just told him that surgery would be out of the question for Tito. They didn't think that he would make it through, so they would have to wait a day for the doctor to figure out the best way to go. And on the next day, the doctor suggested surgery. Never mind what he had said the previous day. Either Tito was going to die without any surgery or he was going to die on that operating table.

He knew as soon as they put him to sleep for surgery that he could be going to sleep forever. After hours of surgery, it wasn't John Patsy "Tito" Francona's time; he came out of the surgery and was soon golfing again, as strong as ever.

If he had wanted to check on his son, he knew the time to do it was during the 2001 season, when Francona was working as a special adviser with his and Dad's old Indians. His responsibilities were different than being on the bench, and he was accountable to fewer people. The closer Terry Francona got to a dugout, the less he worried about himself. Each day was spent pouring all that he had—his energy, his knowledge, and his time—into the betterment of a baseball team. He worked himself to exhaustion wherever he was, whether he had a long history with the players or not. It could also be said, then, that the closer Terry Francona got to a dugout, the closer he was to being at risk. All managers can benefit from a bench coach; it's also safe for Francona to have a personal bench doctor, just to be sure that he is taking care of himself.

After his year working for the Indians, Francona felt that he needed to be on the field again. He liked the scouting and evaluation end of the business, but he was made for the pace of the dugout. He was a subjective man with the ability, certainly, to be objective;

scouting seemed to be the other way around—you had to prove
your objectivity first and then talk about the subjective elements.
Francona was at his best looking a player in the eyes and finding out
his particular story. He was best when he could be there on the field
and in the dugout, places where he grew up, making his observa-
tions about the game.

He left Cleveland in 2001 and landed in Texas as Jerry Narron's
bench coach. He worked with players such as Alex Rodriguez, a
young Hank Blalock, and a banished-from-Boston Carl Everett. The
Rangers weren't very good, and Narron was fired at the end of the
2002 season. Francona was interested in the job, but general manager
John Hart decided to go with Buck Showalter. He had no desire to
stay on staff there, so he went searching for other jobs. Since it was
after the season, he also decided to have minor knee surgery.

There were several reasons Francona had fallen in love with
Jacque Lang 24 years earlier, and none of them had to do with the
fact that she knew something about medicine. He liked her smarts,
and insisted that any wife of his had to be the brains of the marriage, but he never imagined that his wife, the nurse, would spend
a lot of time attending to him. But before she attended to him in
the fall of 2002, she begged him: sweetheart, please, do not get on
an airplane.

He was in Seattle, interviewing to be the manager of the Mari-
ners. He was sweating during the interview, shifting uncomfort-
ably in his seat and trying to stay away from thinking about his
chest, which felt as if a knife was lodged in it. He had pulmonary
embolism, blood clots in his lungs, and he didn't know it. He
didn't know it as he sat with his friend Chuck Cottier that night
during dinner and, abruptly, got up from the table.

"I'm sorry, Chuck, I can't do it, man; you've got to take me to
the airport," he said.

Once he got there, he talked with Jacque, and that's when the begging began: Go to the hospital. Do not get on that plane. He got on anyway, flying all night, and when he landed he did go to the hospital. And that was just the beginning of a medical adventure, an adventure that had him on a shuttle between the hospital, his house, and near-death.

It really did seem that someone was toying with him, playing a sick game of medical roulette, with his number coming up again and again. It would have been enough to stop with a 6-night stay in the hospital, the pulmonary embolism, and being placed on Coumadin, a blood thinner, to prevent additional clotting. He thought he was well on his way to recovery, and he was told not to worry because his blood level, or INR, would be checked daily. His daughter Leah had a soccer game, and he was well enough to attend. As he and Jacque watched it, he started talking about the pain in his knees. He thought it had something to do with being inactive, so he tried to grit his way through it. By halftime of the game, the pain had worsened, and when the game ended, he knew it had nothing to do with being inactive. He thought they might be infected. He was a Francona, and for a Francona man to say anything about pain is serious.

They went to Thomas Jefferson University Hospital in Philadelphia and found that the patient had accurately self-diagnosed, but it took a while for the doctors to agree with him. He was told that the pain in his knees was most likely stiffness from swelling, and that if he had an infection there would be more swelling and he would be complaining of more pain. So now he was negotiating with the experts: they were telling him that the only way they could know anything for sure was to drain the knees, even though draining them was a waste of time; he was telling them to waste their time.

"Drain them," he insisted.

He had been right. There was a staph infection in both knees. He thought he would be given antibiotics and the problem would go away. But he was headed for surgery—eventually. His INR level had not been monitored as closely as it should have been, so he found out that his blood wasn't thick enough for any type of surgery. He waited 18 hours in the hospital until he could have surgery. And when he did have it, he got two helpings of it: his knees were scoped and, 48 hours later, they were scoped again. That led to one more week in the hospital.

What was this? He had six knee surgeries in a 3-week span, and he was supposed to be feeling better. He wasn't. He felt like someone with no boxing experience who had been thrown into a ring with three or four of Philadelphia's roughest boxers. He was beaten, mentally and physically. What was happening? It was November, his kids were doing well in school, it was pro football season, and he was supposed to be on vacation. This was a *vacation*?

It was bad and he knew it. It had all begun so simply on October 12 when he entered Jefferson to have the routine scope of his knees. In November, the entire month had been about pain. He had never been through pain like this in his life. It was so bad, after the fifth and sixth knee surgeries, that when the doctor told Francona he could go home, he responded with, "I'm scared."

He had a right to be. He hadn't gotten out of bed, and his right leg already had an ache. He had eaten a big breakfast and somehow he had been able to slip into his clothes while not leaving bed. He was wearing blue jeans, his favorite pair, getting ready to be sent home, and his leg kept swelling. It was agonizing, even for a Francona man, so the trip home was delayed. Francona was rushed downstairs, fully clothed, for an examination. It was a scene from animation, or something from his kids' video games. He thought, *I wish they'd just cut my right leg off.* He was bleeding fast into that right leg. He didn't know it at the time, but it was a femoral bleed, and in between his anxiety attacks, he could hear one of the doctors shout: "You had better get this motherfucker into surgery right now!"

There was no pain like this. Not the first time he tore his ACL against the Cardinals. Not the second time he tore his ACL against the Pirates. Not the time in 1991, his last spring training, when he was a young man of 32 whose body felt 60 years older. Then he thought it was something to have a body in need of so much attention that the only thing that made him feel better was being up to his neck in a whirlpool. No, no. This was excruciating. He was going to need emergency surgery, and they tracked down Jacque to tell her about it.

They found Jacque at school, participating in a program for one of the kids. They told her that her husband was in emergency surgery, and that she needed to get there as soon as possible. As a mother and wife, your thoughts clash and tumble out . . . *Take care of the kids . . . Get to the hospital . . . Call Terry's father and tell him that he needs to come . . . Oh my God, I can't believe this is happening.*

The problem was that there was no circulation going into his leg, and the blood from his femoral artery was shooting everywhere, filling that right leg with blood, the blood going nowhere. They sliced into his leg, a foot-long incision, and began to save his life. They began surgery and stopped the bleeding, but the doctors felt that what was happening with Francona was so extensive that they packed his leg and continued surgery the next day. He had a Greenfield filter placed in his vena cava, the main vein for return circulation. The filter's function is to catch clots before they enter the lungs.

It would only be fair if the nightmare ended there. It would be fair if Francona, eight surgeries into his baseball vacation, could recuperate nicely, watch his kids grow up, and enjoy the long Thanksgiving weekend. It would be perfect because Thanksgiving had always been his favorite time of year. He remembered all the fun things that happened, like the time he and Jacque invited Frank Coppenbarger and his family over for dinner. The Coppenbargers' son was 3 years old at the time, and as they all waited and waited for Jacque's turkey to be done, they finally got a chance to dig in. The turkey wasn't good, and no one said anything. Except the 3-year-old kid: "This turkey sucks." Those were the things you'd never forget: telling and retelling stories and remembering the football games.

That's what Thanksgiving should have been. What it became was the holiday when Francona was sent home after a week in the hospital, only to experience more pain. He was on an IV, he had antibiotics, and he had no strength. He left his room once, maybe, and didn't have the strength to go to the bathroom. He tried to talk himself into it, it was just a few feet away, but the thought of standing was daunting. He looked at the ceiling in that room, looked up to where he thought God would be, and spoke to the heavens.

"God, please don't give me anything that I can't handle."

But those legs were swelling again. And there was an intense pain in his back. He was told by an orthopedist and spine doctor that the discomfort was due to positioning during surgery. Some positioning: this was brutal. He was suffering so much that he called for Jacque, had her help him get off the toilet—he couldn't do it himself—and corrected her when she said, "I'll get the car."

"Call an ambulance," he shouted.

He had the will to live, absolutely, but there seemed to be a message here. Just when he thought he had to focus on recovery, another condition would arise. So, essentially, he was recovering from three or four things all at the same time. Which is no kind of recovery at all.

Never mind the baseball vacation and a job in 2003. He wanted to live. And walk again. And enjoy the "mundane" aspects of being a husband and father. But this was roulette, and his patience and mettle were being tested. When would he say when? When would he give in? The new problem was that the Greenfield filter was clotted. But now the device in place to catch the clots was too clotted to further do its job. The hospital in Philadelphia had no beds, so he spent two days in a Bucks County hospital, half-consciously looking at the ceiling and waiting for any pain medication.

He was once again that animated figure, his lower body expanding and disfigured. He had gained 30 pounds. After the 2 days in Bucks County, he was taken to Philadelphia and the intensive care unit. Fade in, fade out, take some meds. That was his life; a few times he forgot to breathe. A ventilator was put in his room because, due to his stupor, he would fade out and forget to take breaths. Any day now, he'd be as familiar with the medical jargon as his wife, the nurse, is. He was learning about anticoagulants to dissolve the clots and diuretics to reduce the swelling.

"God," he said, looking at another ceiling. "Didn't I ask you nicely?"

He had, indeed. Even though it didn't seem that way when doctors couldn't give him the answers he wanted to hear. He asked what his recovery time would be like now, and they gave him a vague, "It depends." They talked about developing "collateral circulation." They didn't always say what he wanted to hear.

It depends? That wasn't the answer he wanted. They told him it depended on how strong he was; his recovery was up to him. In the meantime, if he wanted to look at his situation spiritually, he had his answer for the point of this test: his marriage. It was strong before, and it became even stronger. He had been infatuated with Jacque since the day he first spoke with her, but this was beyond infatuation. This was an unshakable foundation, a pyramid much older and more trustworthy than the one young Jacque Lang fell from as a University of Arizona cheerleader.

There were times when she would visit him in the hospital, and just as she was about to leave, the man whom she once thought was too much of a jokester to be serious would say, "Please don't go. I feel so much better when you're here."

He was determined to have his life back. All the Francona men he knew had been strong. He knew Grandpa Francona was strong and full of energy, to do all the jobs that he did. He knew that his father was, because he had felt those hands on him, pulling him through the house after that night of underage drinking. He was strong, too. He knew it. It took some type of strength, mental and physical, to play baseball for 10 years, when at least half of the time he shouldn't have been out there.

At one point he called fellow western Pennsylvanian Ken Macha, the manager of the Oakland A's, and told him that he couldn't be counted on as bench coach in 2003. Macha wasn't going to let him off the hook like that, and it was a good thing, because spring training was a carrot in front of him. He pushed for it. On Christmas Eve, he got strong enough where he could walk the 40 feet from his bed to the nurse station. It was that performance that allowed him to leave the hospital the final time for home—and it had all started so routinely with that arthroscopic surgery in October. He got stronger. He didn't get better as quickly as he got sick, but he could see progress.

Terry Francona doesn't like the idea of pushing his beliefs onto anybody. His prayers are his prayers, and yours are yours. But his prayers were answered; he was not given more than he could handle.

He has several reminders now of what happened then. He has

the scar on his leg. He has a stocking he wears on his right leg to stimulate circulation. He has what appear to be varicose veins close to his navel.

Baseball does become overwhelming to him at times. It's his job, and a job that has its share of stress. But there are few situations on a field that he sees as hopeless, and few situations that he hasn't prepared himself to handle. You can count him out or his team out, but after what he's experienced in hospitals and on fields, he would never do that to himself.

CHAPTER 10

Love, Hate, and Champagne

They're called flyovers. They usually come from fighter jets named Falcon or Tomcat, and they are frequently seen at the beginning of big sporting events. You hear the national anthem and near the end you wait for it: the grumble in the distance, the sudden appearance of the jets, and the amusement and fear of the G force awakening your sternum.

Flyovers. There were two of them on August 30 at Yankee Stadium, but they were different from the others. They happened in the ninth inning instead of before the first. And they didn't come from a jet; they came from a 230-pound Yankees pitcher named Joba Chamberlain. At the moment of the Joba Flyovers, the Boston Red Sox knew what their metaphor would be for the rest of the 2007 regular season: heat. It would be similar to the midday heat in the Bronx—85 on this day—but more personal. It would be confrontational and uncomfortable, and it wouldn't always be as simple as Us versus Them.

So the Red Sox had their metaphor for all of September. That wasn't the problem.

The issue on a Thursday afternoon in New York was that

Chamberlain was not holding a literary device in his right hand when he sent his message. He was holding a baseball, which he could throw at speeds tickling 100 miles per hour. Twice, Chamberlain threw baseballs over the head of Red Sox first baseman Kevin Youkilis. After the first one, players in the Boston dugout swore that they saw Chamberlain glance at New York third baseman Alex Rodriguez as if to say, "What did you think of that?" After the second one, an identical pitch aimed a foot over the first baseman's head, Youkilis threw up his hands as if to say, "What the . . . ?" Chamberlain was thrown out of the game, and the Red Sox had a bitter chaser for their three games against the pursuing Yankees.

They were swept, their division lead was down to five games, and they were being thrown at by a 22-year-old pitcher who was ascending as quickly as they were falling. Chamberlain began the season in Single-A Tampa, was promoted to Double-A Portland, and after an exhilarating stretch of pitching in which he had 125 strikeouts to just 27 walks, the Yankees plucked him from Double-A. Anyone who can deliver five strikeouts for every walk knows how to throw a baseball with precision, so the chances of the ball twice slipping out of his hand were unlikely. Chamberlain threw at Youkilis. Why he did it is unclear, but the act was an official torch-lighting, the beginning of September's heat 2 days early.

The Red Sox knew they would see the Yankees again in 2 weeks, so somebody was going to get hit in one of those three games at Fenway Park. That was the unspoken yet clearly understood law of baseball. The question was, how would the Red Sox travel through those 2 weeks, running or on their knees?

They were the equivalent of the quiet kid sitting in the corner: he doesn't say much at first, but the more he hangs around the more you learn, and sometimes you learn too much. Whatever happened to those peaceful days of double-digit division leads and no big stories?

Now, Manny Ramirez was a story once again. He hadn't played in New York, and his injury, a strained oblique, was just ambiguous enough for people to question how hurt he was. Eric Gagne's performances had been so bad that he was a story even when he wasn't pitching. The two ex-Dodgers, J.D. Drew and Julio Lugo, were stories because they hadn't come close to delivering what was expected.

Since they were all talking points, so were the people responsible for signing and managing them. The first day of September was an aberration for Theo Epstein and Terry Francona. On that day, all anyone wanted to talk about was the kids and how great they were. That was the day a skinny pitcher from Texas, Clay Buchholz, turned his second career start into a 10 to 0, no-hit win over the Orioles. It was a day for Mike Hazen and Jason McLeod and Ben Cherington, all the people responsible for scouting the players, preparing them to play for the Red Sox, and educating them about the extra weight of playing in Boston.

They pumped a lot of time and thought into the best way to raise young Red Sox, so no-hitters were the public pats on the back that they rarely got. They loved to see a game in which second-round pick Dustin Pedroia made a diving play in the seventh to preserve a no-hitter from a first-round pick. They knew what they were doing, but it let everyone else in on the secret when another first-rounder, Jacoby Ellsbury, could make a contribution in the no-hit game and play just as well as regular center fielder Coco Crisp. The first day of the month belonged to Buchholz, but it was a part of them, too, and that's why many of them smiled afterward as much as Buchholz did.

But Epstein knew Boston, and Francona was beginning to know it. They both knew all the talk of kids and development would be quickly pushed aside if the lead dropped below five games. There were certain things that everyone in the city understood, and it started with the division itself. The reality was that if the Red Sox lost the division in the final month of the season, Epstein and Francona wouldn't be recognized as the men who once put a team in position to be up 14½ games over the Yankees; they'd be the ones who couldn't hold a lead when it mattered most.

They both arrived at work each day in September knowing that they'd either be all right with a win or New England's biggest morons with a loss. They were in a city of baseball extremists, quick-trigger lovers and haters, and in a strange way, the atmosphere was addicting. It was high-stakes baseball, and the love of all the heat and action was one of the things Francona had in common with the biggest star he ever managed, Michael Jordan. Some days Francona would steer his black Cadillac Escalade out of the players' parking lot at Fenway, and fans would playfully bow all the way down to the ground at the corner of Yawkey and Van Ness. "Fran-coe-nuh! You the man!" Some days they'd whack the vehicle and hold up their fingers. He understood it and expected it.

"You can't have fans be that interested in a team without getting reactions like that," he says. "I don't think you can have that much passion without also having the capacity to go the other way. There's going to be a backlash. I don't think you can have one without the other."

It would be that way for all of September and whatever the Red Sox had to give in October. It was either win or be shouted at by an all-ages New England choir, featuring grandmas and frat boys alike.

But first there would be more heat.

A week after the no-hitter over the Orioles at Fenway, the Red Sox traveled to Baltimore for a weekend series at Camden Yards. The Orioles starting pitcher was a tower of a man, 6-foot-7-inch Daniel Cabrera. He was not a control tower: he walked more batters than anyone in baseball, gave up more earned runs than anyone in the game, and had a reputation for being volatile when things didn't go his way. They weren't going his way in the top of the fourth inning, when Crisp, standing on third base, began to dance between the base and home.

Cabrera was distracted by Crisp, and it showed when he made a move to the plate and then stopped, resulting in a balk. Now the big man was irritated, and he would take it out on someone a foot shorter. Dustin Pedroia was at bat, and Cabrera's pitch didn't sail over his head as Chamberlain's to Youkilis had; this was a fastball of frustration, fired behind him at eye level.

Players in both dugouts were on their feet, and soon the bullpens emptied for what amounted to a sketch of a brawl. Cabrera, his black Orioles jersey becoming unbuttoned, motioned for several Red Sox to come get him as he was held back by teammates and coaches. Catcher Ramon Hernandez also could be seen exchanging profanities with Red Sox players. Francona would eventually talk with home plate umpire Mike DiMuro and insist that Cabrera be ejected, since DiMuro had initially given both teams warnings. But the manager also found time to visit with Miguel Tejada, one of the players he got to know when both of them were with the Oakland A's.

"Miggy," Francona said, calling Tejada by his nickname. "That was bullshit."

"I know," the shortstop said.

"Miggy, we've got Josh Beckett pitching on Sunday, and he throws real hard."

"I know," he repeated.

After about 10 minutes, the game was back to normal, and the Red Sox won, 4 to 0. Sure enough, on Sunday, with Beckett on his way to his 18th win of the season, an Oriole was hit in the sixth inning. It was Ramon Hernandez.

The division lead remained in a zone, five and a half games, that was acceptable to most New England critics. Anything less, especially with the Yankees scheduled to be in Boston in 5 days, would wake up the choir.

As the Red Sox were beating the Orioles, the New England Patriots were less than 200 miles away, opening their season in New Jersey against the New York Jets. Francona and every other fan who watched parts of the game thought the story was the performance of receiver Randy Moss. He seemed to run effortlessly behind defenders, two, three, four of them at a time, and sprint to the end zone. The Patriots won, 38 to 14, and Moss caught nine balls for 183 yards. But that wasn't the story a day later.

The Patriots had a camera, which they used to record the defensive signals of Jets coaches. The camera was in an illegal position, and as the story gained momentum during the week, it was clear that the Patriots were going to have to pay heavily for the violation.

Each day brought speculation about what the penalty would be. Each day there was talk of asterisks being attached to what the Patriots had accomplished, that three Super Bowl victories should all be questioned, that they were no different than a juiced-up baseball player or some superhuman track star whose "supplements" allowed him to outrun the horizon.

Scott Pioli heard all the news and commentary, mixed together into a media cocktail, and the force of the opinions, from all directions, made him dizzy. He had shared a lot of laughs with Francona as well as some serious discussions. So as the cocktails kept coming, followed by the commissioner's decision to fine the Patriots $250,000 and revoke a first-round pick, Pioli picked up the phone, looking for someone who would just listen. He dialed Francona.

As Pioli began to speak from his office, 30 miles south of Fenway, Francona interrupted him.

"Scott, come on up."

Pioli was unsure. Francona had work issues of his own. A few days earlier, no one in the organization had been able to get in touch with Ramirez. They didn't doubt the severity of his injury, but they were finding it difficult to communicate with him, and between his two agents, neither of them could seem to track him down. How could Pioli ask for anything right now?

"Scott, come on up."

The Yankees were back in town, and Francona would soon have some specialty fan cocktails named after him. It didn't bother him. Pioli was a friend, and when your friends need you, you find a way to help them out. There were certain things in their sports that didn't translate—baseball was fairly open about its sign-stealing and football wasn't—but they could both relate to working for high-profile organizations that are expected to be at a championship level year after year.

It was situations like these that amazed Jacque Francona: how did her husband manage to maintain so many relationships and still do his job so well? One day he is making Pioli laugh when Pioli hadn't laughed much in the middle of what was being called Spygate. One day he is talking to one of his former coaches in Boston and Birmingham, Mike Barnett, who is having a disagreement with another friend, Buddy Bell, in Kansas City. He understands that Buddy probably knows that he's talking to Barnett, so he sends Buddy a text: "I'm just listening!" He is trying to find things for Drew Szabo, his high school golf coach. A former teammate from Double-A needs tickets—tough tickets—but Francona still feels it's his obligation to help.

On the Friday afternoon that Pioli visited him at Fenway, September 14, Francona had to consider how he was going to set up the bullpen. Earlier in the day, Jonathan Papelbon had a migraine so severe that it landed him in the hospital. The closer was treated, told the manager that he was okay to pitch, and asked if he could keep the hospital thing under wraps. Papelbon didn't look like himself, but he said he was ready.

This would be the last Red Sox–Yankees series of the season, and since Boston's lead was five and a half games, the only realistic chance New York had of winning the division was by duplicating the sweep from 2 weeks earlier. But then, a Red Sox sweep of the series, just as they had done in April, would crush any East hopes for the Yankees.

The game began perfectly for the Red Sox. You never get ahead of yourself in baseball, and you slap yourself for the thought against the Yankees, but the game was looking like a win in the top of the eighth inning. It was 7 to 2 Boston, and Francona had the managing essentials at that point: a full deck. In managing, you have those relief cards for specific matchups, matchups that you have played out in your head the night before. He had Okajima to start the eighth, after facing just one batter in the seventh. He had the controversial Gagne available if he needed him. And he had Papelbon, fresh from the hospital, yes, but Papelbon knew himself; if he wanted the ball, it meant he was capable of doing something with it.

What a game. Baseball can turn on you so quickly, so cruelly, that as a manager you learn to take nothing for granted. Nothing. When you manage a baseball team, you pull into a gas station thinking about what you'll do if all 14 pumps are out of petrol. On this night, in this inning, Okajima lost it quickly. In just 13 pitches, he had given up two home runs, a walk, and a double.

Here's the rub about card-playing. A card on the table has to do something; it has to produce some type of action, even if it advances your plan ever so slightly. It turned out that Francona didn't have a full deck after all. Okajima couldn't give him an out, so now the man in the other dugout, dark circles under his eyes, a man who actually played baseball-card games growing up in Brooklyn, was sitting there with the advantage. He knew Francona could do what the sabermetricians—baseball's statistical analysts—wanted, and go to his closer in the toughest spot of the game. Which was that moment. Francona wasn't opposed to that, and when he mentioned it to Epstein when they were just talking the game, the general manager said he loved it when he went to Papelbon in the eighth.

Torre didn't know everything that was in the cards. He didn't know the card had a migraine and had been in the hospital. But Francona had to manage like he would normally, and Papelbon was on his pitching chart. There were two on, none out, the Sox leading 7 to 4. You can't get greedy. Let's say he gives up a fly ball that turns into a sacrifice fly for them. It's okay; you've got an out, you've given up a run, and maybe Pap can get a couple of strikeouts.

It wasn't to be. Derek Jeter singled to make it 7 to 5, Bobby Abreu's double made it 7 to 7, and Rodriguez's single made it 8 to 7. It's not very often that Okajima and Papelbon don't have it on the same night; it will probably take something as rare as Papelbon going to the hospital before the game. A six and a half game lead, which appeared to be a certainty, was down to the angry choir level of four and a half.

"Fran-coe-nuh! You suck!"

Francona often has his car radio tuned to sports talk, so his wife heard all the commentary as she drove home. She argued with the callers who suggested that her husband was an idiot, perhaps the worst manager in the game. "You've got to be kidding me," she said. "He put their two best relief pitchers on the mound and it didn't work out."

No, it didn't. And a Friday-night loss to New York in 2006 became connected to a Friday-night loss to New York in 2007. They were entirely different games, but they were linked by their life spans. The more recent game was with Francona as he left Yawkey and Van Ness—there were none of his worshippers in the streets—and made a right turn onto Boylston Street. It was with him as he got to his house, found one of the kids asleep in his room, and turned on the television to see himself criticized on ESPN.

"He's clearly lost faith in Gagne . . ."

He turned the channel, not in the mood to talk back, not in the mood to say that the intention was not to get Papelbon a six-out save. All he wanted to do was to get out of that inning, and he thought Papelbon was the best man for the job. He *was* the best man for the job; it just didn't develop the way he thought it would. Man. He was racing, wide awake, even though he knew he was exhausted.

After a lot of surfing, he found a Jean-Claude Van Damme movie, *Hard Target*, and it put him to sleep. It didn't cure him, though. He woke up the next morning physically at his house, mentally at Fenway. That game was still on him, still in his head and his heart, and he needed to get it out before he went to work.

"It's like a hitter trying to adjust an oh-for-twenty streak by going ten for his next five—it's impossible to do," he said that morning. "So I don't need to come in here today and make mistakes. That doesn't help. It's one game and it hurt, but it's okay."

He said it, but he hadn't talked it out that easily. Those losses are hard at any time, harder in September, and hardest of all when the players, and the manager, are physically worn out. It's hard when your best reliever has a migraine, your number-three hitter has sore knees, and your cleanup hitter has an injury that will allow him to take batting practice and not play in games. It would get to the point with Ramirez where he would tell the manager that he could pinch-hit, or even hit lower in the order, but not return to his usual cleanup spot. Francona elected to wait until Ramirez could come back and fully participate.

After that tough loss to the Yankees, Francona was asked if he thought he would be perceived differently if fans and members of the media knew all of the things he was juggling daily.

"They can't know," he said. "But you wish that at some point, somebody would just have the confidence to say that this guy probably knows what he's doing. But in this town, I know, that won't happen. So we're trying to take care of people and win at the same time."

The manager would get some of his wish. The day after the terrible loss, Beckett took the mound and handled all of the necessary housekeeping. He shut down the Yankees, and he happened to let the ball slip out of his hands and hit Jason Giambi. It was nothing personal against Giambi, who has friends throughout the Red Sox clubhouse. In fact, Giambi probably knew the pitch was coming. It was just an easy way to answer the two flyovers from Chamberlain.

As for the other piece of the manager's commentary, about wishing someone would say he knows what he's doing, no chance. The lead was shrinking too fast. And the team closing the gap was not located in Baltimore or Tampa or Toronto. The September calendar was starting to taunt; it would hang innocently on the walls of offices and stores, and Red Sox fans would see it as a scare tactic.

On Sunday the 16th, the lead over New York was down to four and a half.

On Monday the 17th, it was down to three and a half.

On Tuesday the 18th . . . That deserves a story.

It's a story that will seem like fiction to those who didn't see it take place in Toronto. It will seem like fiction if you weren't the

Boston manager, checking your e-mail and getting a direct one from Harvard: "Don't pitch Gagne, you IDIOT. You are SUCH a f—MORON!"

The Red Sox were entering the bottom of the eighth in Toronto, holding a 2 to 1 lead. Before the game, Francona and pitching coach John Farrell decided that the eighth would be Gagne's. The reliever, the pitcher no one in New England wanted to see, did well in the beginning of the inning. And then he walked Frank Thomas.

He changed then. At times, he had no control of the ball. He had no one warming up behind him, so this was close to the situation he had seen so many times in Texas and Los Angeles: the game was on him. He gave up a single. He gave up a walk, with some of the pitches elevating to the point where you would have screamed out, "Joba Chamberlain against Kevin Youkilis" if this had been a game of Charades. Just one more out, they were thinking on the bench. If he could get one more out, that would be a huge boost for him, and it would help them know that they had a reliever who could get hot for them down the stretch and into the playoffs.

He walked Gregg Zaun, and a run scored.

He gave up a double to Russ Adams, and two runs scored. The story got better and worse all at once: he did get that elusive third out he was seeking, but only because Zaun, who is not fast, tried to score and was thrown out at home.

The sports radio phones began ringing that night and well into the next day. What the hell was wrong with Gagne? What the hell was wrong with Francona?

On Wednesday the 19th, following a Toronto sweep, the lead was down to a slim one and a half.

To New England, it felt like a bit of fiscal recklessness. What happened to all that money? It should have lasted an entire season, right? The team flew to Tampa virtually assured of a playoff spot, but a spot in the postseason was never in doubt. It was a psychic thing, a New York thing, a thing that went all the way back to first trips to Fenway, first jerseys that said "Rice" and "Evans" and "Fisk." It went back to arguments outside Yankee Stadium, arguments with the hosts on WFAN—arguments that the hosts never heard—fights with visiting New Yorkers in Kenmore Square who didn't laugh when you said "Yankees suck," and they just knew not to laugh because you weren't joking. It went back to the people who didn't get it, who thought that one championship, great as it was, after 86 years would quiet the soul of a region that had been thirsty for that long.

The manager needed that off day on the 20th. He looked terrible. He wasn't getting enough sleep and wasn't eating the proper foods. He was coming down with something, something that wouldn't allow him to eat his food without vomiting. He was hooked up to an IV so he could get something into his system.

He was doing what he thought was right, and he thought it was right to take care of Papelbon down the stretch and to be very careful of what he said about and to Ramirez. He leaned a lot on the assistant principals in the clubhouse, Mike Lowell, David Ortiz, Jason Varitek, and Alex Cora. They all had relationships with Ramirez, some buddy-buddy and some tough love, and they would be able to help if things got too crazy.

The player he truly got to know better during the season was Varitek. He was serious in his preparation, everyone knew that. He would come out of games mentally worn out from all the thinking and preparing he had done with the pitching staff and Farrell. But Francona also got to see a lighter side of 'Tek, a man who could surprise you with his sense of humor.

There was the game in August when Francona had left Fenway and got stuck in the traffic and construction on Route 9. No cars were moving very fast, all the drivers appeared to be aware of it, but there was this jerk behind him, inching close and flashing lights into the car. Francona rolled down his window, ready to yell at the guy, and he looked directly into the smiling face of Jason Varitek.

Now, in Tampa, Varitek wasn't smiling. He talked with Francona about holding a team meeting. Francona told the catcher that he wanted him to understand that he wasn't losing confidence in his team. Varitek shook his head and said he just wanted to say a few things to the players. It was a short meeting, no more than a couple minutes, and it was the appetizer for a piece of what the team had worked for since spring training.

On a Saturday night in Tampa, the 22nd, the team trailed the Devil Rays by a run, 6 to 5, in the ninth inning. Varitek, who had been in a funk at the plate, was facing closer Al Reyes. The talk must have helped him, because Varitek tied the game with a home run. That wasn't even the most poetic storyline of the night, with the man who called the team meeting hitting a home run. The poetry came with a man on base and the former Devil Ray, the man who had tumbled like a cold stock—first in the lineup to last—at the plate. Lugo was still hitting just .239, probably not considered a threat by the Rays.

He turned on the first pitch he saw, lifted it to left field, and confidently jogged around the bases as Ramirez, watching in the dugout, threw his hands in the air.

The Red Sox were going to the playoffs.

They had a toast in their clubhouse later, and Francona and Don Kalkstein, the director of performance enhancement, drove back to the hotel and talked about how much fun winning is, but that the feeling doesn't last long enough. Perhaps they all knew that the divi-

sion mattered more than they had let on, along with finishing with
the best record in the league, and they were holding out for that.

Francona was right about the fleeting feeling of victory. The
next night, there was another loss for the manager to take hard. He
and Epstein, back in Boston, must have seen it the same way in different states; when Francona got off the plane from Tampa, he had
four messages waiting from the GM.

Four days later, they finally got what they wanted. At times it
might have felt like there would be no race at all, and there were
times when the Red Sox felt like they were coming from behind,
even though they were leading the division. All of that changed on
a Friday night at Fenway. The Red Sox had won their game
against the Twins, and there were a few thousand people who
waited to see the end of the Orioles–Yankees game.

The team waited in the clubhouse, and several people, including principal owner John Henry, Ortiz, and Epstein, waited in
Francona's office. They had a comment for each pitch, hoping for a
Yankee collapse. It was 9 to 6 going into the Baltimore ninth, and
the Yankees had Mariano Rivera on the mound. What were the
odds that the Orioles would do anything against him?

Baseball was too weird: the man who tied it up for Baltimore,
Jay Payton, was a former Red Sox who forced the team to trade
him. He didn't accept his role as a fourth outfielder, and things
came to a head in Texas when Francona told him that he wasn't going to travel with the team. And there was Payton with a three-run
triple in the ninth.

Baseball is really weird: in the tenth, the pitcher on the mound
for Baltimore was Chad Bradford, whom the Sox acquired from
Oakland in the Payton trade. He wasn't too special in Boston, but
he was good enough to get out of a bases-loaded jam against the
Yankees.

The game-winner had no Red Sox connection, unless you count someone in Francona's office saying, "He's going to bunt," just as Melvin Mora put down a perfect one. The Orioles won it in the bottom of the tenth, and the clubhouse, covered in plastic, was full of people.

They had beer and champagne, which they sprayed everywhere. They had cigars, which they smoked and passed out. They had Alan Dershowitz, the celebrity lawyer from Harvard Law, taking in the scene and talking on his cell phone. Sitting near his office, with beer on his bald head and a cigar in his mouth, Francona smiled and watched it all. He sat there and took it when Curt Schilling emptied a can on his head, and he did the same when Mike Lowell added some champagne.

Papelbon was a few feet away from the manager. The closer sprinted to the field, wearing black biking shorts and a tight red T-shirt. Sometimes he danced, and sometimes he poured bottles of champagne onto the willing heads of those who stayed for the celebration.

It wasn't all that late, but Francona had already shared a word with Epstein, who hadn't done too bad on his first managerial hire. He had already spoken with his team and congratulated the owners, the scouts, the clubbies, and the policemen. He looked out on that field and said, "I've seen enough." So he walked past the players, the wives, the girlfriends, the security guards, and the beer cans. He walked into the clubhouse, wiped the alcohol off his head, and found John Farrell. The feelings of euphoria are truly fleeting, because he wasn't looking for Farrell so he could spray champagne on him. He wanted to talk about October pitching. The celebration was nice, and the silliness lasted for 20 or 30 minutes. Now he was thinking about the playoffs.

CHAPTER 11

October Sweep

Two weeks earlier, in this same room, Terry Francona had been able to see the future of the Angels and Indians. He did this stuff all the time, especially in his office, where he could put his feet on the desk or stretch out on the leather couch against the wall. Here he'd become a baseball prophet without pretense, a palm reader with no interest in your money. He'd enter this room and do the verbal equivalent of what Tito always told him to do to a baseball: see it and hit it.

He'd been doing this for at least 20 years. When he played with the Reds, he and Buddy Bell would talk baseball at night through clouds of cigarette smoke and shots of vodka. Francona would tell Buddy what was going to happen in the next day's game and Buddy would ask, "How do you know that?" It wasn't the vodka talking; he just knew. (Fortunately, he didn't gamble on his hunches the same way his manager, a guy named Pete Rose, did.) He called it before it happened, sometimes by hours and days, sometimes by months.

It's the reason he was able to say of Toronto pitcher Roy Halladay, a couple weeks prior to a poor May start against the Red

Sox: "He's hurt. He's tough as hell—Eric Hinske says he's off the charts—but I'm telling you he's hurt. His arm slot is lower than normal—he's throwing out of his back pocket. Something's bothering him. You watch: he'll go on the DL soon." On May 11, Halladay complained of lower back pain and had an emergency appendectomy. He was out 3 weeks.

In that same session, Francona spoke of using closer Jonathan Papelbon in the eighth inning: "There are gonna be times we'll do it, it's gonna go haywire, and people are gonna call me a dumbass. I've already warned Theo. It's not always gonna work. He's a valuable weapon, but there's gonna be some hit-and-miss when we go to him in the eighth." Four months later, after a Friday-night loss to the Yankees in which he went to Papelbon, unsuccessfully, in the eighth, Francona would have been called a dumbass all over New England radio stations if it weren't for 10-second delays and the FCC.

He did it again in June, a few hours before his team faced 22-year-old pitcher Matt Cain of the Giants: "Don't believe the record. He's two and six, but this kid's shit is incredible; he doesn't get much run support. I'm looking forward to seeing him up close." Not much run support? How about zero? Manny Ramirez hit a fourth-inning homer off Cain, and that was the only run either team scored that day.

On a Sunday afternoon, 2 weeks before the end of the regular season, Francona was stretched out again on that clairvoyant couch. He occasionally glanced at the football game, Packers–Giants, playing on the small television hanging in a corner. He was one of the guys on these days, talking without worrying about job titles and sound bites. It was 2 weeks before the Red Sox had assured themselves a playoff spot and the best record in the American League. If the Red Sox did have the best record, Francona knew they'd face

Los Angeles or Cleveland in a first-round series at Fenway. He spoke of both teams and unintentionally gave a loose outline of how the pennant would be won.

The Indians were on their way to 96 wins, the same as the Red Sox. They had the top 2 starters in the league, a couple of 19-game winners, in C.C. Sabathia and Fausto Carmona. The Angels were the most aggressive team in baseball, going from first to third in an instant. They created runs that other teams couldn't, and they ran into outs that other teams wouldn't. Their best starter, John Lackey, was an ace against 12 teams, but he saved his worst days for Boston.

Francona: "The biggest thing, I think, is to be home. 'Cause if we have to play the Angels, Lackey has had some rough starts here. We would face Lackey twice, both times here. If we have to go to Cleveland, we'd have to face Sabathia and Carmona twice. That's tough duty anywhere, but I'd rather do it here. Think about the Angels: they came here for three games in April and we beat them, what, twenty-five to three? They can be a hot team and look unbeatable, and they can be cold and look overmatched. How do you know where you're going to catch them?

"Cleveland, man, they're good. They have some weakness in their bullpen. But how do you know if you're going to get there? They might not necessarily get exposed. The one thing that jumps out is this: They're not experienced in the playoffs, and you don't know if that will affect them. But they have good players."

He was full of playoff ideas and opinions then, 2 weeks before he had to be. So when it all became official at the end of September, it was like going over a remedial worksheet. The Red Sox did finish with the best regular-season record, and they were going to begin the playoffs against Lackey and the Angels. The Yankees, who had dominated the Indians in the regular season, were matched up with them in the other first-round series.

For Francona, this was a continuation of high school and college. Then it was never a good time to stop practice. Even at Arizona, where Jerry Kindall's practices sometimes lasted from 1:00 in the afternoon to 6:30 in the evening, Francona never got tired of being around the game.

As a manager, his "practices" were the advance scouting meetings that took place before each postseason series. They went on for hours, usually three, and they included PowerPoint presentations, video examples, subjective examples, cold data, and passionate opinions from the gut. Sometimes there would be as many as 20 people there, from Epstein and the coaching staff to Allard Baird and the advance scouts he coordinated. They would all be there, a bunch of beautiful baseball minds unloading weeks of knowledge into a community pile, and then sifting through the pile for digestible gems to give to the players.

Francona loved it. There was never a lull, there were frequent disagreements, and they usually ended up with a uniform way of attacking a team. Besides, it was baseball. He had such a hunger to talk about it that he had once approached a Red Sox marketing executive with an idea for an off-season TV show: he and a few of the most opinionated members of the media could have a roundtable where they second-guessed him like they did in print and in front of microphones. And then they could sort it out before an audience, seeing if the commentators' ideas were better than the manager's. That would work in Boston, much more so than the cheesy dating shows that the New England Sports Network, in which the team holds an 80 percent ownership stake, sometimes put on the air.

Another subject that would make excellent TV, especially for the How Things Work baseball fan, would be the meetings before the first playoff game. You never want to be too cocky, but anyone who was there saw how lopsided the Angels series appeared to be on paper. These were the cold Angels, broken and lost. Power wasn't their game even when they were healthy, and they arrived in Boston wobbling. Gary Matthews Jr., second on the team in home runs, was out with a bad knee. Garret Anderson, another potential power source, was playing with pinkeye, a condition that had swollen his right eye shut. That left Vladimir Guerrero, a great player, surrounded by rabbits and doubles hitters.

As for the approach to Vlad, the Red Sox knew that they didn't have to pitch to him. In their studies, the scouts found that he was a player who actually benefitted from swings—even swings and misses. The more he swung the bat early, the better he was with it late, each swing seemingly giving him power and increasing his vision. But Vlad was not going to win the series by himself. The Red Sox had too many things in their favor beyond the L.A. injuries.

Ramirez, who had gone more than a month between full games played, was finally back in the lineup. The Red Sox had missed him, but his absence had created an opening in the cleanup spot, and it had been filled well by Mike Lowell. When Ramirez returned to his usual slot, behind David Ortiz, the Red Sox finally found the number-five hitter they had been searching for the entire season: Lowell. The plan was to have J.D. Drew batting fifth and Lowell sixth, but Lowell had been so productive there, delivering too many hits and runs batted in to simply go back to where he used to be. The lineup looked as strong as it had in a month, so it was comically overqualified to give Josh Beckett what he needed for the first game of the series.

One run.

Actually, the lineup was more than overqualified. It was also overworked. Beckett needed just one run to feel supported, and he needed just one inning to get that support: in the bottom of the first against the Red Sox, six pitches into his playoff start, Lackey tried to sneak an inside fastball past Kevin Youkilis and into the mitt of catcher Mike Napoli. But after the pitch, Napoli's mitt was 3 inches from the dirt, in position to catch the ball if it had been there. It wasn't. It was going the other way, a long way, toward left center field and gone for a home run.

Things wouldn't be all that ridiculous for Lackey, compared to what usually happened to him in Boston. He gave up a double to Youkilis in the third, and that stung even more when Ortiz followed it with a home run to right. He walked Ramirez, threw a wild pitch, and had no answers for Lowell, who singled Ramirez home. He wouldn't allow any other runs in his seven-inning start.

Lackey was serviceable in giving up 4 runs; Beckett threw 108 pitches, and if any of them were serviceable, they were disappointments to their master. He gave up a hit to the first batter of the game, Chone Figgins, got out of the inning, and yelled when he got back to the dugout. He always did. He yelled because of a hit, because of a ball that should have been a strike, because of a strike that should have been a *better* strike. So as penance for that hit he had allowed to Figgins, he retired 19 Angels in a row. He never gave those rabbits a chance to run. He was so good in what turned out to be a complete-game shutout that he was getting outs on pitches that weren't even supposed to be his best, second-best, or even third.

Who knew that he had a 96-mile-per-hour cutter? He was supposedly a fastball-changeup-curveball pitcher. He gave Orlando Cabrera that bonus cutter, and people in both dugouts shook their heads. If he was going to be like this for the rest of the month, then they were all acting for the camera, weren't they? Francona would have to act like he had some tough decisions to make in Beckett's starts and the Angels would have to act like they had a chance of hitting his ball, a ball that looked different when it came out of his hand.

The final score was 4 to 0, and one October issue was already solved. John Farrell, who had found a kindred soul in Beckett when they first met, wouldn't have to worry about his top pitcher for as long as the postseason lasted. The man from Texas had the right mix of anger, motivation, and mastery.

The next day, everyone talked about Beckett and how great he had been the night before. Francona was as impressed as everyone else—"that cutter to Cabrera was a joke"—and turned his thoughts to Game 2.

It would be Daisuke Matsuzaka going for the Red Sox, not Curt Schilling, and part of the reason was cortisone. Schilling had been recently given a shot, and he preferred to have as much rest as possible between starts. This would be on Dice-K and Kelvim Escobar, two number-two starters with a penchant for losing it in an instant. Francona thought there was a chance Dice-K would throw a lot of pitches, but "I don't think they'll knock him around. Their lineup is not the same as it was; I think they're where we were a few weeks ago."

As he had mentioned before, being at Fenway could change the way he managed. At home, he could go to Papelbon, even if the team didn't have a lead. "I just think being at home and batting last is a huge deal," he said.

He had been right about Game 2. It had a great beginning, with all of Fenway rising and cheering wildly, pointing at the manual scoreboard. The Yankees had lost the second game of their series to the Indians and were now one loss away from elimination. And there was a story to the game that the scoreboard didn't tell. The mosquitoes that nipped at Tito Francona in the 1960s and Terry Francona in the 1980s had passed the heirloom—nuisance—to their Canadian cousins, and those cousins chased the Indians and Yankees all the way into the 21st century. They were called midges, and they had made the short trip from West 3rd Street to Ontario Street, flustering the talented Joba Chamberlain. As for the Red Sox's Game 2, Dice-K and Escobar were both gone after five, with the score tied at 3.

It was going to be a bullpen game, and a full-strength bullpen game at that. It was time for Francona to play cards with one of the best strategists in the game, Mike Scioscia. Scioscia's teams had finished first or second 5 of the last 6 years, including one year, 2002, when he swiped the daily double of winning the Manager of the Year award and the World Series. In these games, when things were right, Francona always had killer cards that other managers had to account for. As he said, he had Papelbon at home, and he brought him into a tie game in the eighth after Hideki Okajima had gotten the first two outs. Papelbon was a card, yes, and the manager also had the twins that forced you to come up with managerial magic to get by them, Ramirez and Ortiz. Manny and Papi. Two dudes you didn't want to see.

Scioscia had a bigger problem than usual and Francona, rocking away in his red fleece, knew it. The series wasn't even two full games old, and the Angels had gotten Ortiz out just once. And that was a fly ball to center. What was going to happen in the ninth if anyone got on before him? Would the Angels manager pitch to him? Would he walk him and take his chances with Manny?

When the man across from you has to think about these questions, it's a great night to play cards.

The house was against Scioscia, just like in Vegas and Reno and Atlantic City. Where were the cameras? Where was the dealer's secret drawer, the secret card up the sleeve? This was insane: in the seventh, the one power threat that he had, Vlad, was hit on his already sore shoulder by Manny Delcarmen. He had to leave the game. So now he was going to have to manage his team past Papi and Manny without Vlad? Come on; *angels* was just what people called them, not who they really were.

The house came calling in the ninth when Julio Lugo, the number-nine hitter, singled. If the Red Sox stayed out of a double play, Ortiz would have an at bat. The boisterous rookie, Dustin Pedroia, was up and he showed that he also grasped subtlety: He moved Lugo to second with a ground ball, which virtually guaranteed that Scioscia would have to make a decision to prolong the season. Everyone knew it was that serious; did anyone, even in L.A., think the Angels could beat the Red Sox in three consecutive games? Not with Beckett, the exacting and angry guardian, scheduled to be at the Game 5 gate.

So now there was a runner in scoring position, and Scioscia had to bring all the weight he had in the bullpen. He called for Francisco Rodriguez, K-Rod, hoping that he could live up to the nickname. K-Rod was facing Youkilis, and on this night, K-Rod was dealing things that caused Youkilis to be a hair late, just scraping to put his bat on a couple of those fastballs. It wasn't a long at bat: Youkilis went down, swinging at air.

Now it was time for the real Fenway. It was the Fenway that Jacque Francona saw in 2003, when her husband was a bench coach with those A's who were trying to knock the Red Sox out of the playoffs. She was stunned by the wall of sound, trapped in a tiny old park, 37,000 fans pleading and encouraging all at once. They were at it again, pounding the dugout, pounding the walls along the baselines, chanting *M-V-P* and *Pa-pi* and *Let's Go Red Sox,* anticipating something from the giant Ortiz, who had a history of lifting the thoughts from your imagination and bringing them to life. You dreamed home runs and he gave them to you.

But New Englanders aren't the only ones with imaginations; the Angels, remember, aren't that far from Hollywood. Scioscia was aware of Ortiz's history, too, and he made his decision: Ortiz would not beat them. He was walked, for the fifth time in the series.

Even before public-address announcer Carl Beane rolled out his unique pronunciation—*Mah-knee*—of who was up next, the crowd was in rhythm. *Man-knee, Man-knee, Man-knee* . . . Everything from the past was forgiven at this moment. He was out for a month with a strained oblique? Hmmph. Shame on those quack doctors for keeping him out so long! *You the man, Man-knee.* They wore his jerseys and T-shirts, sometimes looked the other way when he played the field, and never turned away when he was at the plate.

They knew the routine. His batting helmet was filthy, the "B" barely visible behind half-dry pine tar and ancient dirt. He'd tap his helmet, spit from the huge wad of chew in his cheek, take a few practice swings, and stare in. When he stood at the plate before swinging, he was everything old-timers had never seen: dreadlocks so long and thick that neither his stocking cap nor helmet could hold them down; baggy pants, so baggy that no one knew just how solid his base was, cast-iron calves that wouldn't move unless he wanted them to; his jersey was a size too big, giving him a sloppy look, but he was a workout fiend, from bench presses to Pilates three times per week with a certified instructor; he wore huge red wristbands with "24" grooved into them, just in case you didn't know who he was.

A Manny swing was a different story. A Manny swing got the old-timers nodding: it was what fathers hoped their kids could mimic, because they hadn't been able to do it themselves. A Manny swing was a rare gift: body in perfect alignment; complete control of every movement, body control that only the world's best modern and ballet dancers understood; head down, hands and weight back. Perfect.

That swing was so perfect in Game 2 that Manny pulled it out of its golden sleeve just once in the ninth. He didn't swing at

K-Rod's first pitch, which was clearly a ball. On the second one, he got what every slugger in the big leagues wants: a perfect swing colliding with a mistake. Most of the time, perfection is able to win, which is what happened on a Friday night at Fenway. He took a swing at a fastball and knocked it deep to left field, out of sight, ending the ball game and, unofficially, the series. He put his hands in the air, and so did the crowd, and everyone seemed to wait for someone else to take the group photo.

One thing Scioscia could have done, maybe, was walk Ortiz and Manny. But not many managers would do that, pushing the winning run to third base with the bases loaded. At some point, you have to bring out your best and take your chances. Scioscia did and it wasn't good enough. It was the story of the short series.

There were a couple of chartered buses waiting for the Red Sox as they exited Fenway early Saturday morning. As they boarded the buses, headed to the airport, they were saluted by crowds who waited outside steel barriers separating them from the players' parking lot. They must have known that they'd be seeing each other soon.

Game 3, the final one of the series, was in Anaheim and it was predictable as well as absurd. There was yet another walk and homer for Ortiz, who finished the series batting .714, another homer for Ramirez, and a 100-pitch, seven-inning scoreless start for Schilling. Each of those things was plausible, but the seven-run seventh was not. It was all bookkeeping after a while, anyway, and the three-game totals—19 to 4, Red Sox—only served to put a number on what many had predicted before Game 1.

Before the first champagne bottle was uncorked, a logical question hovered: who's next?

The Yankees were scheduled to play the fourth game of their series with the Indians the next night. The smart money was on

Cleveland because New York didn't have what either the Red Sox or Indians had; they didn't have a Beckett or a Carmona, an ace other teams feared. The man who was supposed to be their number-one pitcher, Chien-Ming Wang, had given up eight earned runs in Game 1 of the first-round series. And that was his high point. He was miserable in Game 4, lasting just one sorry inning and allowing four earned runs.

Smart money won and the Yankees were gone. The loss would trigger their own series of changes with the departure of Joe Torre and the fading of George Steinbrenner. An era was coming to an end, but Francona would have the off-season to contemplate that. Right now it was time for the Indians.

CHAPTER 12

Comeback Champions

The Cleveland–Boston series pitted upper-middle-class friends from Ohio against wealthy friends from New England. The Indians' payroll was $61 million, not even half of the $140 million-plus the Red Sox were spending.

"I can see a player exactly the same as Theo sees him," says Indians GM Mark Shapiro. "But at times, I have financial restrictions that prevent me from doing things that he can do."

Shapiro chose his words carefully, because he still remembers his first meeting with former NFL coach Bill Parcells. Shapiro and Scott Pioli of the Patriots are best friends, so naturally Shapiro attended Pioli's wedding. Pioli's bride was Dallas Parcells, daughter of the ex-coach. They met at the rehearsal dinner, and Bill Parcells asked the young executive how things were going with the baseball team. Clearly, it was a setup. Parcells didn't want a detailed answer, but he was beginning to get one from Shapiro.

"We've got some guys hurt . . . We're not doing quite as well as we expected in this area . . ."

Shapiro continued to speak, not noticing that Parcells was beginning to turn up his nose. Then, unable to take it anymore,

Parcells interrupted: "Hey, Mark. Always remember this: nobody gives a shit. Okay? They really don't." He explained that ownership, members of the media, and fans really don't care what your problems are. All they want to know is if the team is winning or not. Parcells walked away.

The introductory phrase was still ringing in Shapiro's ears when he went to the men's room later. He was in there, and seconds afterward, so was Parcells. They were side by side at the sink, and Shapiro was looking straight ahead. He didn't want to make any eye contact and get another lecture.

Too bad.

"Remember: nobody gives a shit," Parcells said as he walked out the door.

Shapiro had called Francona after he was fired in Philadelphia and offered him a chance to work in the front office. Francona's other options were what he described as "easy" coaching gigs, and he wanted to do something different. His self-esteem had taken a blow in Philadelphia, but back then he didn't know what he didn't know. Example: he never had a computer while working for the Phillies, and as much as he knew in his heart that his team didn't have all the necessary parts to compete, it's still hard to accept four losing seasons on your watch. Shapiro hired him in 2001, empowered him, and listened to him. When he told Francona that he was looking for a center fielder and explained what the restrictions were, Francona threw himself into scouting. He even made sure that he happened to bump into the players in hotel lobbies, to see what they were like away from the park.

When his mission was over, he had three names for his boss. To show how serious he was about listening to Francona, Shapiro acquired two of the players, Milton Bradley and Alex Escobar, whom

Francona recommended. It was good to be heard, and it was some-thing to watch the brains at work in that Cleveland front office.

But the issue was fire. Francona could sit with you all day and tell you who could play baseball and who could not. That was easy, and it was not managing. Managing was relationships, seeing the same players daily and understanding what got them going. So whether you won or lost, you were still going through something with those players. From a manager's perspective, there was an adrenaline rush to satisfy the thirst of a competitor, and there was a desire to win with people you gave a damn about.

It's one of the reasons he'll always appreciate Schilling, no mat-ter how much the pitcher calls into WEEI, WIP, WFAN, or any other station near you. He'll appreciate him because, in the de-pressing days of Philadelphia, Schilling was still a professional. He'd ask him to be somewhere, and Schilling would show up. He'd say that something needed to be done, and Schilling would go above and beyond to do it.

Not only did the job with Shapiro convince Francona that he wanted to manage again—as well as help him make an early con-tact with Pioli—leaving that job and returning to the field put him in contact with people who have made him a much stronger leader. His next job after Cleveland, in 2002, took him to Texas, where he worked with DeMarlo Hale.

"D, if I ever get a managing job again, I'm taking you with me," he told him. "You're good." He liked the way players trusted Hale, he liked his preparation, and he appreciated how self-critical he was when he made a mistake on the field.

In Texas, he also met the sports psychologist Don Kalkstein, who had worked with the Rangers and the Mavericks, and he was liked by athletes from the city, the suburbs, Australia, and Africa.

Francona watched him, too, knowing that he'd have a place for him if he ever got another shot.

In 2007, his chance of getting another championship was being blocked by the Indians and Shapiro, the GM who had helped make him championship-ready in the first place. He had introduced him to Pioli, too, so he tried not to make it too awkward before Game 1 in Boston. Pioli was in Francona's office, speaking with the manager and his son, Nick. At one point, Francona looked at Pioli and said, "Aw, get out of here. I know you have to go over and talk to Mark. He's your best friend."

Pioli made the walk from the first-base dugout—with Nick Francona—toward the third, to speak with Shapiro. There were so many connections in the series, from the front office to the field, that it was dizzying. Coco Crisp and Ramirez were former Indians in Boston; Trot Nixon and manager Eric Wedge were former Red Sox in Cleveland; Farrell and Francona were teammates in Cleveland who went on to work in front-office jobs for Cleveland and now coached together in Boston.

Just like in the previous Game 1, there wouldn't be much an opposing team could do with Beckett. This time, he did have good reason to yell about something after the first inning. In their scouting meetings, the Red Sox had noticed that Travis Hafner was a half-second late turning on fastballs, so that was a note Farrell could take to his pitchers. What the scouts didn't know was that there would be a strong wind blowing out to center, and if Hafner was a little late on the fastball, contact could still mean a home run. So Hafner got his home run, Beckett yelled, and the Red Sox scored the next eight runs of the game.

By the sixth, there was media talk of taking Beckett out early and having him fresh to bring back in the fourth game instead of the scheduled fifth. That subject would come up a lot in the next week, and it was one of the things that turned Francona into one of the most cursed names in town. But that was for later. Game 1 was a fulfillment of the Leather Couch Prophecy: the Red Sox won 10 to 3, and Sabathia, a durable and dynamic pitcher in the regular season, had his second bad start of the playoffs.

The series got no clearer after the second game, and didn't really take on its personality—panic, for New Englanders—until after the fourth. But in Game 2, the Red Sox were able to strip the mystique away from Carmona, just as they had done with Sabathia. Carmona had control problems, and he had reached 100 pitches without completing five innings. That was good.

It also helped Francona to know, for future late-inning card games, that he had taken a huge one, Rafael Perez, out of Wedge's hand. Perez's earned-run average during the regular season was 1.78, and if you combined his ERA with Rafael Betancourt's 1.47, it was still lower than closer Joe Borowski's, which was over 5. So they were so exceptional in setting him up that he often had wiggle room for his adventurous ninth innings.

The other side of the Game 2 story was that Schilling was having his problems, too, and he lasted just two outs longer than Carmona. It was the game that many had expected, although no one saw Carmona and Schilling checking out of it so early. It was tied at 6 in the 9th, and going into the top of the 11th, Francona had already used Papelbon for two innings, and he'd gone to Manny Delcarmen, Okajima, and Mike Timlin before him.

He was going to have to go to Eric Gagne.

Red Sox fans had long given up on him and couldn't wait to see him leave town as a free agent. He was more unpopular than Drew, who at least had won some games for the team. "He's a lot better than he's shown here," Francona said of Gagne. "He happened to struggle at a bad time, in the wrong place." Gagne made people jumpy; his apparent discomfort made others uncomfortable, and there were groans when the bullpen door opened and he was seen running out of it. He did run out in the 11th, and he wasn't all that bad: he got Casey Blake to strike out, and he gave up a single to Grady Sizemore. When he walked Asdrubal Cabrera, his night was over, and he had to know he'd be the target, along with Francona, if the Red Sox didn't get out of the inning.

They didn't get out for what seemed like an hour. The Indians scored seven in the top of the 11th to pull away, and run back to Cleveland with a tied series and, with the next three games in Ohio, home field advantage.

This wasn't the Cleveland that Francona and Farrell knew nearly 20 years ago. The ballpark, Jacobs Field, was just 13 years old, and it had fans who wanted to sit in it. Francona and Farrell had played in a drafty football stadium, built on a landfill by Lake Erie. George Brett once said that Cleveland Stadium was so empty that he could hear the few fans there teasing him about hemorrhoids. If you didn't hear conversations, you heard the drum of John Adams, echoing off 70,000 empty seats.

When the Indians moved to Jacobs Field, they left the football stadium but brought the football crowd, a crowd that frantically waved white towels and cheered each pitch, as if their team needed a stop on third-and-long. It was quite an atmosphere. When the Indians were able to take Games 3 and 4 in front of that crowd, you could see a bit of hope dilating the city's sad eyes, eyes that had been deadened by Michael Jordan, John Elway, and—a half-century earlier—Willie Mays. The Indians hadn't won a World Series since 1948, the Browns hadn't won a championship since 1964, and the Cavaliers had never won a thing. There were towels waving in the city because championship flags were not. It was an area that had no problem celebrating excellence with Halls of Fame—pro football and rock 'n' roll—but it had teams that didn't win titles and inspired you to sing the blues.

After the Indians won Game 4, 7 to 3, they were one game away from the World Series. The cities were swirling with opposite energies, with Boston ironically acting out a phrase—"Round up the usual suspects"—that was coined by Epstein's grandfather, Philip, a cowriter of *Casablanca*. Epstein himself was on the list. So was Francona. Drew. Lugo. Crisp. There was talk that the smallest and boldest Red Sox of them all, Pedroia, was overmatched at the top of the lineup—he was hitting .188 through four games—and needed to be moved down.

Francona was up on multiple charges, starting with his decision to stay with Beckett as his Game 5 starter. The critics wanted him to use Beckett a game earlier and shift the rest of the rotation around that move. He was unwilling to do it for a couple of reasons. One was that Beckett had a cut on his right index finger and wouldn't have been the same pitcher that he would be in Game 5. The other was philosophical.

"My goal is never to just prolong a series," Francona explained. "My goal is to win it."

He thought the move-up-Beckett crowd was shortsighted, thinking of only one game and not the complexion of the entire series. He knew Beckett on regular rest would be good, and all it took was one victory to change the negativity.

As for Crisp and Drew, Crisp was the likely candidate to be moved. He was hitting .188, the same as former teammate Sizemore, but he was having no impact on the game at the plate. He was a whiz in center, but was that enough to keep rookie Jacoby Ellsbury out of the lineup? It was a nonissue to Francona going into Game 5 because he knew he was going to use reserve outfielder Bobby Kielty against Sabathia, because Kielty had great numbers against him. He was not willing to change two-thirds of his outfield positions for one game, so Crisp started again—and submitted one of his worst offensive games of the playoffs.

Crisp was able to struggle, though, and not be a headliner the next day. The towel-waving quieted and the World Series parties were put on hold because Beckett, performing like the best pitcher in the game, was at work again. Before he went to work, the sly Midwesterners tried to play with his head. The Indians invited country singer Danielle Peck to sing both the national anthem and "God Bless America." The attractive brunette was a good choice, based on merit alone. But she wasn't chosen on merit: the Indians claimed it was just a coincidence that Peck happened to be Beckett's ex-girlfriend.

They should have known better. She's a great singer, not hitter. There were two dramatic moments in Game 5, and neither one of them helped the Indians. In the bottom of the third, with Ortiz on first, Ramirez crushed what appeared to be a home run off the top of the right-field wall. As he is wont to do, Manny admired his work, only to learn that the ball hit a yellow strip atop the wall. The ball was in play. The admirer, sheepish now, was stuck at first. He did drive in a run, but he should have at least been on second.

Francona ran out to argue with the umpires, even though he knew that Ramirez should have been running. Francona, standing between first and second with his back to first, got the attention of Indians first baseman Ryan Garko. "Hey," he said to Garko. "Look over my shoulder and tell me if Manny is still on first." Garko nodded and put his glove to his mouth to hide a laugh. "Yeah, I thought he was still there," Francona said, shaking his head.

In the fifth, Beckett got tired of yelling at himself and picked someone new. He chose veteran Kenny Lofton, who apparently bothered the pitcher by placing his bat down when he thought strike one should have been ball four. After Lofton flied out to left, he ran to first and cut across the field to exchange words with Beckett. The bullpens emptied. Players stood around, and the umpires sent everyone back to their places.

There was no more drama, except for Clevelanders to wonder what happened to Sabathia. He still hadn't put together a postseason start worthy of someone who was the likely Cy Young Award winner. Was he struggling for the same reason Cy voters would applaud him—the 240 innings pitched? Or was it something that Francona mentioned way back in September—inexperience?

The Red Sox won Game 5, 7 to 1. Beckett gave up a run and five hits, and struck out 11. There are few certainties in sports, but Beckett was one in October 2007. He was not going to lose, to the Angels, to the Indians, or to the Rockies if the Red Sox were fortunate enough to get that far.

Back in Boston, the feeling was that the Red Sox, trailing three games to two were now the favorites. Schilling was scheduled to face Carmona in Game 6, and Dice-K would go against Jake Westbrook in Game 7. The logic was that Schilling, a terrific pitcher in the postseason, would display enough stuff and know-how to get by the nervous kid. And in Game 7, the Red Sox could always call on the emergency team, which included Beckett, if they ran into trouble.

Fenway is often called a magical place, which it is, with its old-style pinball machine angles, expanse of green, and quirks, like seats not facing the field, that let you know that it is not from this era. It is magical and old, but it is modern America in the sense that it's not obsessed with institutional memory. This can be a disheartening thing when you have a body of work that is good, and are suddenly out of Fenway favor because of a patch of bad performances. It can be good, or at least amusing, when you have done poorly for a season and then are forgiven—a curtain call?—with a single surprising act.

And so that was the big story, the only real story, of a runaway Game 6. Before it ran away, there was tension in the park from the knowledge that the season could be over in a few hours. The tension intensified and peaked at game time. Minutes later, plans were being made for Game 7.

It started in the Indians' first, when Schilling tore through the first three batters in 11 pitches, getting Hafner, hitting .130 in the series, on strikes to complete the 1-2-3 start. Carmona, though, didn't appear to have any confidence or ability to locate. He quickly loaded the bases, giving up singles to Pedroia and Youkilis, and walking Ortiz. He almost got out of it when Ramirez struck out and Lowell hit a fly ball that wasn't deep enough to score a run.

At the plate: J.D. Drew.

Many of the people at Fenway had watched him come up short all season when they had expected so much more. He had been so average that even his average season stats—.270, .373 on base, 64 RBIs—seemed inflated. They weren't good stats, but he hadn't been that good, had he? This was on Theo. You heard that a lot after Game 4, with J.D. often the final point in the debate over whether Epstein was a good GM.

What Epstein loved and fans hated about Drew was his approach at the plate. He was a skeptic, daring a pitcher to throw three strikes on him. He did a lot of watching, and there were many times when he took a seat without moving the bat with aggression. The hope in Game 6, with Carmona scuffling, was that Drew could salvage the inning and draw a walk.

He was well on his way, three balls and a strike, and all the crowd needed to see was another ball. *Don't swing if you don't have to, J.D.* Turns out that he had to. The pitch was just too fat, catching too much of the plate. He got it and he put a charge into it, driving it to center field. Carmona's shoulders slumped, right there on the mound. Grand slam, J.D. Drew. The park of forgiveness, giddy and stunned, called for him to come back out because they weren't through thanking him.

This series was going to Game 7 because the Red Sox scored six more runs in the bottom of the third, leading 10 to 0. Carmona left and was replaced by new mop-up man Perez. The reduction in Perez's role had meant an increase in Betancourt's. It could play a factor in Game 7, which always had a chance to be the ultimate bullpen game. When the Red Sox won, 12 to 2, no one called for Drew to be replaced, for Pedroia to drop down, or for Francona to get a clue. In fact, there were a lot of people sounding like managers going into the seventh game. They wanted to know who was available in the bullpen and the minimum number of innings they could get out of Dice-K.

But in moments like these, who cared what the fans thought? Francona had always maintained that managing was not a Top 40, pop-music type of industry. You didn't go with what was hot, you went with what was right, if indeed you had a process that let you know it was right in the first place. It all went back to the first interview he had done with Epstein; he had a process. You don't panic when an entire region is trying to figure out who's most to blame—before a series is over.

If they had known how he felt before Game 4, they would have panicked that he wasn't panicking. Then he played cribbage with Pedroia and talked with Ortiz in the manager's office at Jacobs Field. Before the game he spoke of how relaxed he was. "It's as relaxed as I've ever been, going into games," he said a few hours before his team lost Game 4. "I love this time of year. I love the games. Sometimes you have to be confident in your preparation, relax, and wait for the outcome."

That would have been a controversial quote immediately after Game 4, the emotion of being up or down 3 to 1 clouding the judgment of both Cleveland and Boston. But prior to Game 7, it had a different interpretation, even though the speaker didn't change; the situation did. He was relaxed when he was down 3 games to 1, and he was relaxed when the lights on the stage changed, bigger, brighter, hotter for Game 7.

He called it before it happened: the Indians were a good team, extremely talented, but maybe they would perform differently under these circumstances. In the first few innings of Game 7, nerves didn't seem to be a factor for either side. The Red Sox had three runs off Westbrook by the third, but the pitcher didn't give in. He forced the Red Sox to ground into double plays in the first two innings, with one of the double-play balls scoring a run. Another run scored on a Lowell sacrifice fly in the third. It was 3 to 2 Red Sox after five, when Francona felt that he had gotten all that he could out of Dice-K: six hits, no walks, two earned runs.

The manager had Beckett available, but he didn't have to be that radical; he had two pitchers in his bullpen, Okajima and Papelbon, just like the old days of June, who hadn't given up a run in the series. If he needed to, he could use them both for the remaining 12 outs and drink even more champagne. Okajima had no problems in the sixth, 1-2-3, and was a witness when the Indians' season collapsed in the seventh. When Francona had spoken of inexperience, he presumably meant the inexperience of kids named Sizemore and Jhonny Peralta and Carmona. Did Lofton, the oldest Indian at 40, cross his mind?

Lofton made a play, or didn't make one, that turned out to be the biggest of the series. Never mind that he shouldn't have been on base in the first place: he popped up to shallow left, and Lugo waved off Ramirez because he thought he had it. He dropped it. Lofton was on second with one out. He could have scored easily when Franklin Gutierrez singled to left. The ball hit the third-base photographers well and rolled into left. Ramirez had essentially conceded the run by the time he got to it, but third-base coach Joel Skinner had held Lofton at third.

Was it the player's fault? The coach's? As all of Cleveland thought about it, along with wondering how Jordan had been able to score over Craig Ehlo at the buzzer to win a series over the Cavaliers . . . and how Elway had driven his team from its own 2 to tie an AFC championship game against the Browns . . . Casey Blake grounded into an inning-ending double play.

It was 3 to 2, and it was going to get bad fast for Wedge and his team. He had gone to Betancourt once too often, and finally the Red Sox were going to make him pay for it. Wedge must have felt he was all right with the matchups in the seventh. Betancourt was facing the bottom of the Boston lineup, which on this night included rookie Ellsbury batting eighth, Lugo ninth, and then back to the top with Pedroia.

Soon it was a case of one rookie helping out another. Ellsbury reached on an error, and the player from Arizona State whom Jason McLeod loved so much and campaigned for, Pedroia, put that big swing to work and had himself a two-run homer. It was 5 to 2, and it was going to get even worse for Betancourt the next inning. He threw it, they hit it to center field: Lowell, Drew, Varitek, Pedroia . . . they were pelting him, and when he left it was 9 to 2. When a fresh-faced kid named Jensen Lewis replaced Betancourt, Youkilis hit a home run off him.

It was okay to say it aloud, even though the game was not over. The Red Sox, on their way to an 11 to 2 win, were going to be hosting the Colorado Rockies in the World Series. When they finally got done hitting, and were able to hold in smiles for three more Cleveland outs in the ninth, the Red Sox, for the third time in less than a month, cracked open a few dozen cases of champagne. They threw another public party for their fans, complete with beer and cigars and the pennant that had seemed so unlikely a few days before.

Francona celebrated with the players, but he was thoughtful during these times, too. He liked to win, and he loved to win with people he respected. There was obviously Millsie, who didn't have to worry about hurting his feelings and didn't get sensitive when Francona snapped during games. There was also Hale, whom Francona trusts so much that their first conversation about the job went something like this:

HALE: What do you need me to do here?
FRANCONA: Coach your ass off. I know what you can do. That's
    why you're here.

In Farrell he has a pitching coach who has the skills to be a general manager. He didn't know much about Luis Alicea as a coach, and he grew to respect the way Alicea taught Pedroia to turn double plays. He laughs when he speaks of Magadan, because the hitting coach is someone he never sees; you're not supposed to see the hitting coach much if he's doing his job, hanging around cages and computers.

The season was coming to a close, probably sooner than they all imagined. The Rockies had been the hottest team in baseball for a month, but the story hadn't changed: whether the opponent was a baseball team or a baseball front office trying to bring about nostalgia—or disappointment—regarding an ex, Beckett was going to be better than anyone else's number one. So if need be, he was worth three victories in a series.

All he needed was one. He began the World Series the same way he had begun the first round and the league championship series. The Red Sox scored 13 runs, the Rockies scored 1, and a nation could see where this was going. It was going to be a championship that everyone in the organization could feel, from ownership for spending the money, to the baseball operations people for knowing how to spend it on the minor leagues and scouting. The organization got a win in Game 2 when a piece of information from those long advance scouting meetings was put into practice.

By the World Series, the Red Sox scouts had analyzed everything there was to know about all teams in baseball, including their own. They knew that the scouting report on Papelbon was that he didn't hold runners well on base, and that the Rockies' Matt Holliday would take a sizable lead against him. So when Holliday got on in the eighth, with Papelbon on the mound, Millsie gave a signal to Varitek: Tell Pap to throw over to first.

The signal was delivered, Papelbon threw over, and a scoring threat was snuffed. Two college friends, from 30 years back, looked at each other and one of them—Millsie—sniffed and smiled. It was out of character for the man who never celebrates himself, but it was the World Series, and it was a lot better than the old days. They both remembered them. They remembered playing golf each year at the end of the season at Saddlebrook, and each year they'd run into a fired pro coach. One year it was Wayne Fontes, the former coach of the Detroit Lions, and one year they looked around and wondered where the fired pros were. They laughed; it was *their* year. They had just been fired by the Phillies.

Philadelphia had made Francona wonder. The experience made him better, but it cut deep, too. "It's not just sour grapes," he says, "but I never felt that I belonged there." People would walk up to him on the street after he had been fired and ask him why he was still in town. He went to an Eagles–49ers game when Terrell Owens was still with the Niners and he was on the field near a few Eagles players. They were interested in baseball and he wanted to hear about football. They talked, but they were drowned out by a chant that they thought was "T.O. sucks . . ." They looked around and saw no T.O. They were talking about him: "Tito sucks . . ." It just wasn't the place for him.

Going into Game 3 of the Series, in Denver, he wouldn't allow himself to think of stats that the people of Philadelphia never thought he'd achieve. He was 6 and 0 in the Series, and two wins away from his second championship in four years. He tried to stay in his normal routine, joke with the players, and abuse Pedroia in cribbage. He then wrote Pedroia's and Ellsbury's names at the top of the lineup and watched them combine for seven hits. If you add the hit of another rookie, Dice-K, it was eight hits from the rooks in a 10 to 5 win.

The guys tried to talk about it the next day, but Francona wouldn't let them. Lowell and Pedroia were in his office, and they talked about how crazy it was that the season could be over that night. Francona changed the subject. He didn't want to think about being 8 and 0 on the Series stage, where the elite card players congregate, or the possibility of an eight-game winning streak in one postseason and a seven-game streak in another.

With that said, he was happy to see the look on Jack McCor-mick's face during the Series. McCormick's official title was trav-eling secretary, but Francona wasn't much for official titles. He trusted McCormick, a former Boston cop who seemed to know anything and everything about the city. McCormick had pa-trolled Kenmore Square, the Back Bay, and the South End in the

1970s and 1980s, when those areas weren't nearly as trendy as they are now. Francona knew McCormick had witnessed a lot of painful Red Sox history up close, and he was glad to see the Commander—his nickname for McCormick—glowing with the team on the cusp of another championship.

There are many people in Boston like McCormick. These are people who can remember exactly where they were when Carlton Fisk hit his famous home run in 1975. "I was working a detail that night at the park," McCormick says. They can remember where they were for Bucky (bleeping) Dent. "Section 14," McCormick says. Of course, everyone remembers October 2003, but as a planner, McCormick has an even tougher story: He had to be sure that someone was taking care of putting up protective plastic in the Boston clubhouse for the inevitable champagne celebration in Yankee Stadium. The champagne changed directions quickly with one out in the eighth inning.

On October 28 in Denver's Coors Field, Francona was making New England history, simply by being himself. Under his guidance, the old Boston/Red Sox paradigm was being gutted and retooled. People like McCormick were about to see a second title, when 5 years earlier they had begun to fear they would never see one. It didn't take a screaming manager to get the job done. He had a knack for being in control yet not overreacting to things his players did.

A perfect example was the All-Star break. He had warned Josh Beckett that he wouldn't get back to Boston in time if he went to Texas after the All-Star Game. Beckett said he wouldn't be late, but Francona was right and Beckett didn't get back in time. The pitcher was apologetic, and he felt even worse that he had young Jon Lester with him, a pitcher who watches everything Beckett does. Francona accepted the apology and gave Beckett his punishment: five dozen golf balls, a dozen each for the coaching staff. You can't treat all players like that; the trick is figuring out how each player accepts responsibility.

With Beckett, Francona quickly noticed how good he was with his teammates. In baseball, players are aware every day when they are being watched—or not—by starting pitchers. It's a small thing, but it's important to the players. No starting pitcher is as supportive as Beckett.

"He's smart," Francona says. He chuckles. "Is it a coincidence that he gets great run support? You tell me."

The manager is neither self-promoter nor Hall of Famer. The man with the winning formula is from a town many New Englanders have never heard of; the man who oversees titles never dreamed of managing. As a boy, he would have been content to *play* for the Red Sox or anyone else. Do 9-year-old boys pretend to be managers in pickup games? Terry Francona didn't, but on the last Sunday in October, he was a few outs away from being the most successful manager in the 21st century.

He sat on the bench in Denver, rocking, as Papelbon took the mound in the ninth. He felt sick as he saw a player named Jamey Carroll send Ellsbury to the wall for the second out of a one-run game. He quickly had managerial thoughts: *If we don't pull this one out, we have Beckett coming back tomorrow, but we don't have Pap and Okajima available . . .*

Soon he could relax. Soon he could let the players enjoy the celebration and the subsequent party at the Palm Restaurant. He had his family in town, and on the night the team won its second title in 89 years, he was going to do something wild: Yahtzee. They were all there in his room at the Westin Taber playing Yahtzee: Nick, Alyssa, Leah, Jamie, Jacque, and Terry.

Let other people talk about the importance of 2 in 4 years, and let whomever get the credit for the success. It's because he manages a rich team? Cool. It's because of something else, from someone else? It's all right.

"I'm at peace with myself," he says. "I feel fine, physically. And I don't go back and relive the whole thing."

Sometimes, though, it's hard to get the season out of your system. Three or four days after the World Series, Francona was still having trouble sleeping. When he did sleep, he would wake up in a panic, wondering who was pitching tonight and nervous that he hadn't gotten in all his preparation. The season was over, he was supposed to be relaxed, yet he was still cranky and irritable.

He told Jacque that he needed a couple days to be calm. He packed a bag, made sure he had a Lee Child book that he had been reading, and headed south to Orlando. The general managers' meetings were going to be there in a couple days, so he would spend a good day and a half by himself, reading and decompressing. It was exactly what he needed; by the time Epstein got to Florida, Francona felt great.

They were both in Orlando, a week after the World Series, staying at the same hotel. Francona told Epstein to meet him in the hotel bar so they could have a few beers and watch the Patriots–Colts game. As Francona waited for Epstein, he sat at the bar and heard a couple of people saying how tired they were of seeing the Red Sox on TV. At first he thought someone was playing a joke on him, but these folks had no idea that they were trashing the Red Sox within earshot of the Boston manager. He laughed to himself and then met up with Epstein.

They had reached the point in their relationship where they didn't have to have constant chatter to be comfortable. Francona liked that Epstein had lived up to his promise in his original interview. Then, he had told the manager that they should be able to have intellectual debates—and bar debates, too—without putting a dent in their relationship. They certainly had that. Francona was confident that he could have an opinion completely different than the GM's and Epstein would still listen carefully.

So they sat there, eating and drinking, not saying anything for 5 or 10 minutes at a time. Finally, with the edginess of the season out of his system, a thought suddenly hit Francona. He looked over at the man who hired him and said, "Theo, can you believe that we won the World Series again?" They laughed and toasted and drank to that one: the grandson of a piano player and the grandson of a screenwriter, collaborating on a brand-new Boston script.

Manager of the Year ... or Not

Long before October 18, 2007, Terry Francona understood how thankless the job of baseball manager can be. On that night, he was in Cleveland, his team one game away from playoff elimination. He was completing his fourth season as the Red Sox's manager, so he was familiar with the rules: If the team lost, it was his fault; if the team won, he was merely the store manager who made sure the lights were on and all employees were in attendance.

Francona's team won that night, Game 5 of the American League championship series, and didn't lose for the remainder of the '07 postseason. A few hours before the start of Game 5, Francona was able to see the ultimate in managerial under-appreciation: Joe Torre, owner of four World Series titles with the Yankees and 12 playoff appearances in succession, was offered a $2 million pay cut and incentive-laden contract from his bosses. The richest team in baseball seemed to believe that it was also the most talented and motivated team in baseball, so another loss in the first round of playoffs—for the third consecutive season—was deemed to be unsatisfactory. Torre rejected the offer and eventually signed with the Los Angeles Dodgers (replacing, ironically, Grady Little).

Francona didn't have a lot of time to think about it while his team was still playing, but when he got a moment he acknowledged the change in Red Sox–Yankees dynamics. He traded messages with Torre, telling him how much he enjoyed competing against him and wishing him well in his next job. In 2008, Francona would begin strategizing against Torre's successor, Joe Girardi. There would no longer be the same combination of civility—"How's your dad?"—and hyped quarreling, which all amounted to a standstill. Over 4 years, Torre and Francona met 82 times, with Torre's team taking 42 games and Francona's 40.

In 2007, Francona finished fourth in Manager of the Year voting, trailing three men, Torre, Mike Scioscia, and Eric Wedge, who he either finished ahead of in the division or head-to-head with in the playoffs. During his four-season, two-title run in Boston, he has yet to receive a single first-place Manager of the Year vote. The way he sees it, not receiving credit is not a bad thing; his managing style is to actually put his hands on the wheel less. He prefers humor over humiliation, stage left over the spotlight.

"We don't try to overdo it," he says. "We don't want to over-manage or over-coach. We try to create an atmosphere where players want to do the right thing."

It's not an approach that will launch a manager into national superstardom, or even into the "Who's the Best Manager in Baseball?" debates.

"If you think about it, the Manager of the Year awards are silly," he says. "There are guys doing great jobs who aren't winning a lot of games. When Gene Lamont was in Pittsburgh, I thought he was one of the best field managers out there—and his teams didn't win a lot [they lost 93 games twice]. But I felt that his teams always played better than their talent.

"Or what if you have a young team and the players are getting better? Doesn't that mean that someone is doing something right? It takes a strong manager to have the patience to stay with them when they're not playing well."

He had young players who got better playing for him, and he had veterans who produced after he stayed with them longer than fans wanted. The big reward was winning the World Series, but nothing tangible beyond that. After the season, the Red Sox made a couple of contract commitments. They re-signed Series MVP Mike Lowell and pitcher Curt Schilling. When the Pirates were looking for a manager and inquired about pitching coach John Farrell, the Red Sox responded by giving Farrell a new contract. A contract extension was discussed with Francona during the first half of the '07 season, but those talks never got serious enough for a new deal to be put in place.

If any of his Red Sox bosses are waiting to hear him say how great he is at managing, that wait just might rival the historic one New England had between 1918 and 2004. It's not Francona's style. Torre has a better contract than he does, which makes sense, but the Reds topped $3 million for the season for Dusty Baker and the White Sox extended a contract averaging $2.5 million per season to Ozzie Guillen. Francona's not close to either number.

So the 2008 season could be the manager's last in Boston. Even with that knowledge, Francona went into the off-season campaigning for someone else.

"With all his experience, I don't understand why Millsie can't get an interview with somebody," he said of Brad Mills, his bench coach and friend of 30 years.

He knows that he'll be in a good situation with some team, whether it's in Boston or elsewhere. With Boston's resources, he'll always have a chance to do what he was doing on a sunny Tuesday afternoon, October 30, in Boston. That day he was part of a Red Sox caravan that rolled through the streets of Boston, from the Prudential Center to Boston Common to City Hall, waving to thousands of celebrating fans. The first time he saw a Boston World Series parade in 2004, Francona looked into eyes, weepy and red, ecstatic over the first Boston title in 86 years. In 2007, the eyes were wide and bright, happy and expectant. Francona rode along with his coaches and smiled at all the scenes, including closer Jonathan Papelbon in a kilt, singing and dancing along with a Boston group called the Dropkick Murphys.

He smiled for the region, for the city, and for the players he had grown so close to. He even took a moment, ever so brief, to smile for himself. Winning was great, for sure, but so was having a life in baseball, which is all he had ever wanted.

Afterword

In early 2008, Terry Francona's relaxing moments lasted, literally, as long as a scoop of ice cream. His temporary home, from January to March, was the Homewood Suites in Fort Myers, Florida. He knew he could always rely on an impeccably made bed and the complimentary ice cream in the hotel lobby, but that's where the daily certainties ended. His baseball year began with a surprise, and that would become the norm for the entire season.

That's not to say all of the surprises were bad. Actually, the first one was refreshing. Francona, who was entering the final season of his contract as Red Sox manager, had been trying to negotiate an extension for most of the previous summer. As summer turned to fall and the Red Sox became 2007 World Series champions, Francona expressed skepticism to his friends. He knew that his employers liked and respected *him*; he just wasn't sure how much value they placed on his position. No Boston manager in nearly a century had won two championships in four seasons as he had, and that achievement was going to result in tremendous leverage for the manager. The surprise came when he didn't have to use it. After the season, Francona's agent gave the Red Sox an opening number, and that number was not laughed off the table. A new deal was reached in February, and Francona's average annual salary, about $4 million, made him one of the best-paid managers in the major leagues.

Barely a month into his contract, he found himself leading one of the boldest protests of his professional life. The standoff came at the perfect time, before the final spring training game of '08, because it was yet another hint of the oddities that were to come. The issue began innocently enough, with Francona talking to one of the employees of his former organization, the Oakland A's. The Red Sox and A's were going to begin their season in Tokyo, and while Francona didn't like what an abbreviated spring training and early Opening Day in Japan would do to his team, he understood why Major League Baseball wanted to do it. As he talked with his friend from Oakland about the trip, money came up.

"Do you realize our coaches aren't being paid for the Japan trip?" the friend said to the Boston manager.

"Really?" he replied. "I wonder why not; ours are."

As Francona walked away, he began to understand the unlikelihood of two teams going to Tokyo and only one of its coaching/support staffs being compensated for the trip. He knew that if the A's weren't being paid, then that meant the Red Sox weren't, either. And that was going to be a problem since he had spent a portion of his off season, haggling over the details of the trip. He had been assured that his staff would be taken care of, and now there appeared to be a change of plans. Francona spent the next few hours with a cell phone to his ear, trying to get an answer to his questions. When he still didn't have the answers he wanted the next morning, he was furious. The Red Sox were scheduled to play the Toronto Blue Jays at noon in Fort Myers, in a nationally televised game, but as players and coaches talked about what was happening, the players came up with an ultimatum: if the coaches weren't going to be paid, the players were going to boycott the spring game and refuse to play in Japan.

It didn't take long for the dispute to reach baseball commissioner Bud Selig.

"Even though you believe in your principles and doing what's right, you get a little nervous when you're talking to the commissioner and telling him that you're not gonna play," Francona said. "I mean, this is not some Beer League. There was a lot at stake."

After a short delay, the Red Sox were given the assurances that they were looking for and, several hours later, they were off to Tokyo. Since they were thirteen hours ahead of their fans in Boston, the Red Sox started their first game of the season at the same time many commuters were trying to escape morning traffic. First pitch: 6 A.M. For followers of the Red Sox, there was nothing strange about seeing a box score in which Manny Ramirez had the winning hit, which is what happened in Tokyo. Few people would have guessed, though, that the popular and generally serene Ramirez would eventually string together a few off-field events that would be discussed as much as the outfielder's memorable home runs.

Ramirez had arrived at spring training in good spirits, uncharacteristically speaking with the media and repeating aphorisms from the bestselling book *The Secret*. At 35, two months shy of 36, Ramirez was said to be in the best shape of his career. He was preparing for a new contract, just in case the Red Sox were unwilling to exercise one of the two $20-million-per-season option years they held for Ramirez. Yet he insisted that he wasn't thinking about his contract and actually wanted to end his career in Boston.

The Red Sox had long rationalized their enabling of Ramirez.

He was a once-in-a-generation diva, unpredictable and often un-reliable when he was off the stage, and a leading man who shone brighter than the spotlight itself when he was called on to perform. He was a ferocious worker—on his terms. Because he played for the Red Sox, members of the team looked at his flaws and euphe-mistically scrubbed them into "quirks." Because he played for the Red Sox, many fans took the specifics—Manny is not running hard to first—and reshaped them until they all fit under an in-nocuous banner: Manny Being Manny. Francona had become an expert at reading Ramirez's body language and knowing when to give his gifted slugger a day off. If not, he was aware that Ramirez could very easily take a "summer vacation" that could last any-where from a day to a month, which is what many in the organiza-tion suspect happened late in the 2006 season.

Even though there were unofficial Ramirez Rules for everyone in the organization to follow, the Red Sox were ill prepared to deal with the Manny of 2008. He was upbeat and approachable as late as early June. But on the same night that the Red Sox brawled with the Tampa Bay Rays at Fenway Park, Ramirez took excep-tion with the way the always animated Kevin Youkilis reacted af-ter making an out (cursing, occasional helmet toss) and took a swipe at him in the dugout. The incident was quickly airbrushed with boys-will-be-boys cliché. Less than a month later, before a game in Houston, Ramirez became frustrated with the team's traveling secretary, Jack McCormick, and pushed him to the floor. When word of the incident leaked, the Red Sox once again moved to sweep away the details, with as little damage as possible. But the episode troubled Francona deeply. It wasn't just that Ramirez had assaulted a team employee, and it wasn't just that the employee happened to be 64 years old. It was that McCormick may be as close to Francona as anyone in the organization. One of the first times Francona came to Boston, McCormick picked him up from the airport and gave him a tour of the city. It's McCormick who often tells him the best places to go to dinner, in Boston or elsewhere, the best routes to take when the main roads are jammed, and the best people to talk to, for issues large and small.

When Francona's friends in baseball heard about the incident and saw the very vague, corporate statement from the Red Sox, the calls, texts, and e-mails came in a hurry. The consensus: Francona should have said more. He agreed with them. It was clear, despite the public statements about these things happening to every "family," that the Ramirez–McCormick incident couldn't be forgotten easily in the Boston clubhouse. Ramirez was changing, too. He began referencing his contract more. On a West coast trip in mid-July, he decided to have a protest very different than the one the entire team had in March. Ramirez didn't want to travel from Los Angeles to Seattle with his teammates and had to be talked into it. Once in Seattle, he claimed that he couldn't play.

Something had to happen. Ramirez was convinced that he stood to earn more money as a free agent, so he didn't want the Red Sox to pick up the option years on his contract. Meanwhile, there was a baseball season going on, and at times, the players were distracted by the man who could really help them win. If he wanted to play. And that was the issue: he didn't want to play for the Red Sox anymore. After an embarrassing 9-to-2 loss to the Angels, a game in which the Red Sox had four errors, it was time to make a move. Francona and general manager Theo Epstein weighed the opinions of many players, and most of them agreed that it was time for Ramirez to play for a new team. On July 31, with Boston three games out of first place, the team initiated a deal that sent Ramirez to the Dodgers, prospects to the Pirates, and a left fielder named Jason Bay to Boston. Bay wasn't as dynamic a hitter as Ramirez, yet he was far from a liability at the plate, in the field, or in the clubhouse.

Not only would Bay help the Red Sox get into the playoffs, he became part of a reenergized team, a team that found a way to advance to the American League Championship Series. It was also a team that had the manager saying something in October that he never would have imagined in June: "This group has given me some of the most fun I've ever had in baseball. We've just got a great bunch of guys."

Acknowledgments

Before I thank all the smart and generous people who obviously made this book possible, I want the first words to go to a special man, Larry Whiteside, who is with us now only in spirit. I had the pleasure of working with Larry at the *Boston Globe* for 10 years, and in that decade it was clear that Larry was not like the rest of us.

He was as graceful as he was stylish, and his generosity was as large as his hometown of Chicago. He was not in journalism to see how quickly he could get himself onto a star track. He was an assist man, getting more satisfaction from furthering the careers of others rather than his own. Larry made it his mission to get more African Americans involved in journalism, and as scant as their overall numbers are today, they would be infinitely smaller without the persistence of Larry. His constant willingness to advise younger journalists is worthy of a position in the Hall of Fame, but that's not why he'll be honored in Cooperstown, New York, in the summer of 2008. He loved baseball, he covered it well, and he agonized over many of the teams, specifically the ones in 1978 and 1986, which are referenced in this book.

I'd like to thank Larry for setting high professional standards, both in his reporting and in his counseling. Elaine, you had a wonderful husband, and Tony, you had a great dad. He deserves all the applause—and more—that he will receive in Cooperstown.

There are dozens and dozens of folks who nurtured this project from idea to book, so I'll separate them into readable categories so they won't be lost in the roll call.

William Morrow: I knew Mauro DiPreta was a great editor because I had worked with him before. I didn't know that he had so much patience. He clearly saw through my requests, very early in the process, for just a little more time. He knew that meant I was going to be late with the manuscript and ruin all his major holidays. He showed great restraint in his e-mails, never resorting to the dreaded and angry ALL CAPS messages. Mauro and Jen Schulkind embraced the story from the beginning and helped me refine it.

The Story: Any glaring omission from this book can be attributed to my limitations as a writer. Terry Francona was remarkably open about some personal moments in his life, with an openness that's a lot more difficult than when talking about the games. But Francona talked about the games, too, and was gracious when I asked, repeatedly, for him to go over topics that had already been discussed three or four times. I was a daily presence in his life for a year, and he never stopped to say, "Wait a minute: where in the hell is this thing going?" If I asked, he usually answered.

One thing should be clear in the book, and if it's not let me try again: Francona is an extremely bright manager who is uncomfortable talking about how smart he is. In New England, the only time his intelligence is mentioned is when fans claim that he hasn't any. But he has expanded the local championship template, proving that his subtle style can work in his sport, just as the opposite works for Bill Belichick in his.

There are two stories that perfectly illustrate Francona's trusting and understated nature. The first one is really a recurring one: Everyone in the Red Sox clubhouse understands that Francona's wallet is a community wallet. Players and clubbies short on cash have been known to peel away a couple twenties from the manager's wallet, knowing that they have to replace the cash "at some point." Sometimes they tell him days and weeks later, "Hey, I took fifty bucks out of your wallet; I'll be getting that back to you." So Francona has no problem leaving his wallet in view, never fearing that it will be stolen.

The other typical Francona story took place in late January, when he sent a text message that read, "Had dinner with the President last night. Pretty cool." No bragging, no exclamation points, no breathless reports. *Pretty cool.* With some prodding, he revealed what he had for dinner (steak) and that the president wanted to talk baseball and specifically wanted details on what it's like to manage Manny Ramirez.

All of the Franconas were helpful during this project. Tito, Jacque, Nick, Alyssa, Leah, and Jamie: thanks for the interviews, time, and brownies (Jamie). Several of Francona's friends and colleagues helped me fill in several blanks with their interviews and stories: Theo Epstein, Mark Shapiro, Ben Cherington, Scott Pioli (thanks for the Earth, Wind & Fire CDs), Bill Giles, Frank Coppenbarger, Greg Fazio, Drew Szabo, Jayson Stark, Joe Castiglione, Jerry Remy, Dick Williams, Gabe Kapler, Jack McCormick, John Blake, and Michael Jordan.

Sources: I relied on several books for information and context, especially for the chapter titled "New School." *The Bill James Guide to Baseball Managers* is a terrific book that traces the evolution in managing from 1870 to the mid-1990s. Long before Bill Plaschke became a full-time—and exceptional—*Los Angeles Times* columnist, he collaborated with Dick Williams on the shockingly candid memoir *No More Mr. Nice Guy.* Williams opened up to Plaschke and left no doubt why he was a feared manager in two countries and three decades. Other key books were *Weaver on Strategy* (Earl Weaver and Terry Pluto), *Chasing the Dream* (Joe Torre and Tom Verducci), *Moneyball* by Michael Lewis, and *The Man in the Dugout* by Donald Honig.

I don't know what I would have done without baseball-reference .com; if you can dream up the baseball scenario, you can find it on that Web site.

Finally, New England has a highly skilled stable of baseball writers, from Providence to Boston to Portland, Maine. I'm amazed by the high volume and high quality of work the men and women on the baseball beat are able to produce daily.

Friends, Family, and Colleagues: My family, immediate and extended, which has always been loving and supportive: Mom, the Soberanises, the Shakurs, the Johnsons of West Akron, the Robinsons, the Prestons, the Alleynes, the Smiths, the Owens, the Godwins, and the Sales. Ray and Gloria Hammond, and the entire family at Bethel AME Church, have been kind, brilliant, and welcoming; I thank God for leading me to your ministry. My brothers in Geekdom at WEEI: Dale Arnold, Jon Wallach, Rene "Cape and a Cane" Marchando, James Stewart—I love all of you; you all helped the previous three years go by quickly by making work so much fun.

There are many others to thank as well: Basil Kane, an expert on cigars, soccer, and literary deals; Holly Driscoll (one of Manny's Pilates instructors), Jen Flynn, Kim Flynn, Corey Bowdre, Jordan the Boxer, "Larry David" Carona, Uncle William Alston, Jeff Robinson, Geespin, and Point Park University (crazy underrated journalism program).

Rest in Peace: Samuel Jackson Cravanas, Boopie Sales, Alice Roper, Larry Whiteside.